VICTORIA UNBUTTONED

Lillian Gray, ca. 1899.
Gray Family Collection

VICTORIA UNBUTTONED

A RED-LIGHT HISTORY OF BC'S CAPITAL CITY

Linda J. Eversole

TOUCHWOOD

TouchWood Editions
touchwoodeditions.com

Copy edited by Renée Layberry
Cover and interior design by Sydney Barnes
Front cover images: (Top) Lillian Gray. *Gray Family Collection*; (Bottom) Wharf Street looking north from Fort Street. *City of Victoria Archives, M07068*
Back cover image: Lillian Gray. *Gray Family Collection*

CATALOGUING DATA AVAILABLE FROM LIBRARY AND ARCHIVES CANADA
ISBN 9781771513388 (print)
ISBN 9781771513395 (electronic)

TouchWood Editions acknowledges that the land on which we live and work is within the traditional territories of the Lkwungen (Esquimalt and Songhees), Malahat, Pacheedaht, Scia'new, T'Sou-ke and W̱SÁNEĆ (Pauquachin, Tsartlip, Tsawout, Tseycum) peoples.

We acknowledge the financial support of the Government of Canada through the Canada Book Fund and the Canada Council for the Arts, and of the Province of British Columbia through the British Columbia Arts Council and the Book Publishing Tax Credit.

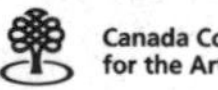

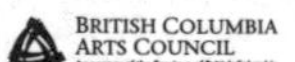

The interior pages of this book have been printed on 100% post-consumer recycled paper, processed chlorine free, and printed with vegetable-based inks.

Printed in Canada at Friesens

25 24 23 22 21 1 2 3 4 5

For my daughters, Machala and Cheryl,
resilient spirits, empathetic hearts

Contents

INTRODUCTION 1

1: FURS, FORTUNES, AND FANCY WOMEN 15

2: CAPITAL, CONFEDERATION, AND "COMPANY LADIES" 42

3: LANDLORDS, LADIES, AND LOST SOULS 57

4: BROADS, BUILDERS, AND BANKERS 80

5: IMMIGRANTS, IMPOSTERS, AND INMATES 97

6: DETECTIVES, DEPORTATION, AND DEMIMONDES 115

7: THE REFORMERS 145

EPILOGUE 170

ACKNOWLEDGEMENTS 174

ENDNOTES 176

SELECTED SOURCES 189

IMAGE CREDITS 201

INDEX 203

Introduction

Victoria Unbuttoned, salacious as it sounds, is the result of my examination and exploration of the lives of those deemed unfit for recorded history. When we challenge assumptions about those who have come before, we challenge ourselves to see our own lives through the lens of history, without sentimentality or prejudice, and find sympathies that know no distance of time.

I am intrigued by Victoria, British Columbia—a place that has gone from being a sleepy, staid town to a charming, colourful, lively city. It's a city I would want to visit if I did not already live here. Over the past five decades I have seen Victoria grow and change while retaining a sense of its heritage. I have been privileged to observe the creation of many culturally significant works of art originating in the carving shed at Thunderbird Park. I walk down streets in the old town, which still have wooden block paving and historic structures. Along the way I have felt the presence of the people who have come before; this has driven me to learn all I can about their lives.

One group that is absent from a variety of historical records is the poor—particularly women in poverty, who were disadvantaged in a patriarchal society. The stories of their lives—especially of those who lived outside the "norm"—offer the present-day researcher greater depth of feeling and understanding of the times.

I was born in Qualicum Beach and spent my earliest years in a little cabin on Buller Road; my father ran the old wooden gas station on the main road along the coast. I was lulled to sleep nightly by the sound of the waves on the shore, and I am happy to say my childhood cabin still stands among more substantial houses. We had a resident hermit, Giuseppe Roat, about whom many years later I would write, and on occasion my mother and I rode the wonderful E&N train to Victoria. It was an idyllic start to a young life.

Much of my life has been spent in Victoria, save for a childhood in New Westminster and Edmonton. I have also had various sojourns, particularly in England where I worked in archaeology; this experience fuelled my passion for history. Indeed, history is well entrenched in my DNA: My family takes pride in our roots, which sprung from Scotland, Northern Ireland, Upper Canada, and the Anabaptist Eversoles of Swiss origin. These roots were the source of family stories of travel to new lands and pioneer life.

In the early 1970s I was thrilled to get a position at the newly opened BC Provincial Museum, now the Royal BC Museum, in the History division. My path also led to employment with the Victoria City Archives, with Ainslie Helmcken, a grandson of pioneer doctor John Sebastian Helmcken. Later I worked at Point Ellice Historic House, the BC Golf Museum, the Steveston Museum, and the Sooke

Region Museum. I spent six months at the York Archaeological Trust, mostly cleaning human bones from a Saxon burial. Interspersed with these great jobs were many travels to foreign places, usually in service to some historical passion—Russia's czars, Rapa Nui's magnificent statues, Oman's lost city of Ubar, and Tunisia's troglodyte homes (used to depict Tatooine in the first *Star Wars* movie). From Europe to Japan, the Cook Islands to Chile, and India to Egypt, I relentlessly followed my passion for history—a passion that is still not quenched.

Between my travels I managed to land a dream job as a research officer for the Heritage Branch of the BC Government. Twelve years of diverse assignments took me around the province and through decades of time to research all manner of properties, individuals, and locations to help facilitate preservation.

My work included research in government documents, letters, journals, newspapers, and photographs. I travelled to where the materials were—some were in archives, others were in offices, and some were held by individuals. I spent hours sitting on floors in government offices going through heavy leather-bound ledgers from land titles, surveys, and vital statistics. I tromped through deep snow to photograph an abandoned fur trade cabin near Nazko. I posed beside the world's largest truck in the coal fields of the Rockies. Impelled by the desire to understand the diversity of people's lives, I would find myself driving my elderly car through the

Cariboo backroads to Quesnel Forks to explore its early log structures built by Chinese miners during the gold rush. I gazed in awe at the wonder personified in the ancient poles of Haida Gwaii, and I was privileged to be included as an observer of the ceremonies returning culturally significant objects to their rightful owners. As I worked and explored, it became abundantly clear that the personal stories of individuals are the heart and soul of any study of history.

I met many people along the way, all of whom impacted my thinking and approach to the past. Whether conversing with an elderly Indigenous resident of Keremeos about the building of the local Grist Mill (now a historic site) or a hundred-year-old former bartender who knew the early saloons of Victoria well, I found that interviews with pioneers, Indigenous peoples, and knowledgeable historians brought new information and insight and led to a fuller understanding.

These diverse experiences, which I feel privileged to have had, were born of the ideas and work of many individuals—some revered, some forgotten, some flawed, some heroic, but all human. Along the way I found myself wondering how much I could learn about the individuals whose lives were deemed unremarkable and, through a myriad of circumstances, lost to history. As I was well versed in the types of research materials available, I dived more deeply into exploring primary source material including census records; directories; birth, marriage, and death registrations;

wills and probates; military service records; and land and chattel transfers.

It was Ainslie Helmcken, Victoria's founding city archivist, who first answered my query about women in criminal activities and made mention of an intriguing woman by the name of Stella Carroll, Victoria's pre-eminent brothel keeper of the early twentieth century. What began as an idle question led to years of compiling research, writing letters, applying for copies of primary documents; it even led to a trip along the Pacific west coast—from Washington to California, family in tow—to uncover her story. As luck would have it, I was able to spend some time with John Carroll, one of Stella's family members. He provided me with numerous photographs, family stories, and leads to material from other family members, when we met in his charming townhouse filled with antique furniture, some of which came from Stella's brothel.

Stella's life opened a gateway to understanding the business of brothels and prostitution, and insight into the complexity that went beyond a single establishment. It also brought to light individuals whose only records were seemingly in police and court documents and newspapers. I gathered and put aside information on the history of the business of prostitution in Victoria—more specifically the lives of individuals who were involved, predominantly American women. In later years I would follow an easier research path via digital access to records; these revealed even more primary information, allowing me to employ forensic genealogy to track present-day descendants. In this way I used skills already honed over the years when tracing individuals for legal purposes for government agencies and law firms.

In all this I gained a greater understanding of unconventional lives—not necessarily criminal or immoral, just unconventional. By sharing my findings in this book, I hope to shine a light on the lives of women who followed a specific path, sometimes from need and sometimes from choice. Their involvement in the sex trade does not define them but is merely a part of their story. For some such as Stella Carroll, Lillian Gray, Emma Johnson, and Christina Haas, the sex trade was a big part of their lives and a profession they followed. For others, such as Grace Trachsler, Martha Gillespie, Nettie Sager, and Dora Son, it was less a vocation and more a way to cope with illness, addiction, and a fear of living in poverty. For Edna Farnsworth and Alice Young, it was an unfortunate chapter that ended short, tragic lives that had hardly begun.

All of these women's stories are very different. I regret that I was limited, both by my own lack of familiarity and by the sparseness of available primary sources—save for the observations and racist rants reproduced in court reports and news stories—from profiling in any great detail the experiences of women from Indigenous or Chinese communities in Victoria. I was, however, able to include a few details on the life of Kateka, an Indigenous woman whose story intersects with that of local policeman John Westrop Carey (see Chapter 1).

Sexual commerce is not usually top of mind when talking about the growth of a city. In fact, as illuminated in the saying "the world's oldest profession," sex work is an ever-present economic sector that consistently defies attempts at abolition or regulation. Where people gather and settle, the business will always be present.

The west coast of North America was coming into its own in the mid-1800s because of gold—particularly the California Gold Rush of 1849. The coastal location was desirable for many other reasons, but this event brought the type of sojourner that in time would profoundly impact the Pacific Northwest region and lead to the eventual creation of the Province of British Columbia. Early exploration and the already-established trade in furs, with the resulting establishment of forts and trading stations, brought increasing interest from individuals driven by a desire for adventure and new opportunities. This grew to greater numbers a few years later when the exhausted California goldfields gave way to discoveries farther north along the Fraser River in what was then the Colony of British Columbia. Communities along the coast were inundated with great economic opportunities, and aside from the obvious needs of transportation, shelter, and supplies, there was an impetus for permanent settlements to grow and thrive.

A rush to capitalize—not just for settlers, but for Indigenous populations too—meant local expertise and knowledge of the land was also a valuable resource. Thus came the expectation of mutually beneficial trade and alliances for traders and Indigenous peoples. However, this expectation would fall far short for the Indigenous peoples who lived in the area as well as those who travelled to interact with the HBC. In terms of sexual commerce, the imbalance of power was exposed and carried on through attitudes of settlers who did not partner well with people they thought of as inferior, despite being dependent on their labour. Daily interaction could lead to friction, and the lack of a common language beyond chinook jargon—the commonly used pidgin trade language spoken in the Pacific Northwest—meant only basic communication between disparate individuals. As far as sexual contact, an increase in population and in particular the introduction of alcohol and dance halls (also known as "squaw halls," a pejorative term in settler parlance) led to a necessary establishment of law and order, based on the British system. The influence of religious proclaimers determined to bring others to the God they worshipped had considerable power on the establishment of order in the growing community—as did their beliefs on morality. These newcomers made the rules and administered them as they saw fit.

The fort settlement grew into a community, then a colony, then a city; along with this growth came the evolution of the quasi-legal business of prostitution and the attendant changes in law and its application, morality, and ideas of reform. In the beginning the members of this rudimentary society were dependent on each other for everything. Entries in the *Fort Victoria Journal* reveal a community working together to build the fort, clear land, build fencing, plough fields, and run supplies from Fort Vancouver on the Columbia River (near present-day Portland, Oregon). Local women participated in agricultural work alongside the men and partnered with them in living arrangements. By 1848 the Reverend Monsieur Veyret was determined to take control and convince the populace to follow a godly life. He was looked on with some contempt, for his arrival coincided with the spread of diseases previously unknown to the local population. In time he did persuade some of the workers—many of whom were Metis who had been transferred to Victoria from Fort Vancouver to work—to formalize their liaisons. As the *Journal* recorded:

> *Mon^{r} Veyret has married eight of our Canadians to ~~their~~ Indian Women.*[1]

With the onset of the gold rush, the agricultural community became a transport and supply centre for gold seekers, and the population grew dramatically. A larger and more formalized policing and judiciary was put in place, and the little settlement of Victoria became home to a variety of individuals from all over the world, many arriving from the US seeking a more lucrative future. In 1861 Hector Smith, from California, was made chief of police not long after his arrival. He had this to say in a communication about the conditions related to the white inhabitants and the Indigenous population:

> *The lowest class of Society from Victoria infests the coast, supplying spirits to the Indians and carrying on other nefarious pursuits, to the great demoralization of the Indians, and to the serious danger and annoyance of respectable settlers.*[2]

This was supported by the Reverend Alex Garrett, Principal of the Indian Mission at Fort Victoria. In his government report, he used language and descriptions that would not be tolerated in the present day. His words below clearly illustrate racism and division:

> *The moral and social condition of all the Indians resident at Victoria is extremely bad.*
>
> *This arises mainly from the following causes:*
>
> 1. *From the natural tendency to evil of the savage mind, the natives copy with extreme facility the vices of their civilized neighbours.*

> 2. *They are drawn toward ruin with resistless power by the strong temptation held out to them in the gains of prostitution, and the ease with which they obtain a large amount of intoxicating drink.*[3]

Garrett did not seem to have any use for any of the inhabitants of the colony, generally, but one comment would ring true: Alcohol was destructive for many of the residents, whether Indigenous or settlers, and its effects would be felt for generations to come. Garrett was already seeing the terrible effects of diseases, such as measles and smallpox, brought into a community not equipped to withstand it, and he tried to introduce inoculation programs with mixed results. In the end, alcohol and disease would decimate the Indigenous population.

As the fort grew to a colony in 1849, then a sizeable settlement in 1858–59, dance halls, saloons, hotels, and small brothels were scattered throughout the community while religious leaders tried to create some sense of decorum. Clashes arose, not just over morality and prostitution but the general air of debauchery—alcohol again the fuel. More non-Indigenous women appeared in the colony, some as wives, but others also looking for opportunities or dealing with their own difficult circumstances. Nettie Sager and Martha Gillespie, who we will meet in early chapters, were among the women who caused a stir in town. Although their stories were quite different, both were well known in their day.

The transition from open debauchery to some discretion in operating small brothels came with the ability to obtain more substantial places to work. From the 1870s, buildings were constructed with more permanence in mind; rental opportunities were there, and for some the chance to purchase a well-located house near areas where workmen resided. Broughton Street was centrally located and adjacent to carriage works and later the Victoria Transfer Company. It had several medium-size houses to rent and one to buy. Also, the barrack-type annex of the stables was made available as a brothel property to rent and was well suited with its number of small rooms.

Broad Street too was a prime location, and even though the cabins gave way to brick buildings, rental properties such as Duck's Building were available; madams such as Vera Ashton, Marval Conn (AKA Emma Johnson), and Stella Carroll eyed these properties, anxious to create upscale carriage houses with a higher-class clientele and substantially greater profits. Their stories in Victoria began in the 1890s, and in the case of Stella continued to the onset of the First World War.

Many brothel keepers learned their business in San Francisco's high-end resorts, particularly from the famous madams Jessie Hayman and Tessie Wall, who set a standard to which other madams would aspire. Stella Carroll, Lillian Gray, and Christina Haas had ambitions; they knew their business and all aspects of running a parlour house. Others such as Della Wentworth and Henrietta Morgan had less grandiose aspirations but also learned much from their days in the notorious "sin city" that was San Francisco; they set up shop on Broughton Street.

Los Angeles madam Lee Francis (AKA Beverly Davis) collaborated with "Serge G. Wolsey" (the pseudonym of journalist Gladys Adelina Lewis) on the memoir *Call House Madam*.[4] While undoubtedly dramatized, this memoir gives insight into the costs of high-end establishments in the heyday of San Francisco in the 1890s and early 1900s. Lee was "turned out" by Jessie Hayman when just a teenager and had plenty to say on how things were run. According to *Call House Madam*, brothels ran under one of two systems: The first was a boarding house arrangement where women paid for a room, board, and expenses while the madam provided a clean and well-decorated establishment. The second system was a percentage house where the madam also supplied food, liquor, and the services of additional staff such as housekeepers, bouncers, and musicians. In exchange, the madam took a percentage of earnings, anywhere from 25 to 55 percent; the madam also earned money through liquor sales. Women in these houses were expected to dress well, with a wardrobe to impress on the streets and tantalize in private.

Lower-level prostitution could range from a woman perched in her window in various stages of undress and soliciting customers, to women working in their own premises and offering services at much lower prices, between two to five dollars.

Today most, if not all, of the small buildings that housed brothels have been wiped out in the development of the city of Victoria. The only remnants are large brick buildings that were originally rented to madams or independent operators along Herald, Johnson, and Fisgard Streets. Duck's Building on Broad Street is one remaining vestige of the sex industry; here, the second and third floors ran as a high-end establishment from 1892 to 1905. With the disappearance of suitable buildings and the pressure of moral reform, the sex industry gradually went underground, disappearing into discreet hotels and private residences after the First World War. Despite such pressure, street prostitution also began to flourish once again, and the dangers of such a life led to many tragic endings.

The women profiled in this book are just a few of many who came to Victoria seeking a life that would provide them comfort and companionship. Some succeeded, and others didn't. To understand the business of prostitution, it is necessary to explore the lives of those who practised it and to examine their relationship to the wider community around them.

Chapter One

FURS, FORTUNES, AND FANCY WOMEN

IN 1843, TO STEM AMERICAN EXPANSION INTO BRITISH-HELD territory, the Hudson's Bay Company (HBC) established Fort Victoria, enlisting James Douglas from the company's depot on the Columbia River to locate the site and begin construction. In time Douglas was made chief factor of the Pacific Coast operations; he would oversee the many stages of development of the new community.

Fort Victoria. *Victoria City Archives M09017*

The centre of the fur trade was more northerly, but it was thought expedient to have a depot on British territory that was still well placed to service traders coming south, particularly the Haida and other Northwest Coast groups bringing sea otter furs. In time this trade dwindled. A *British Colonist* editorial in 1861 suggested northern Indigenous traders shouldn't be allowed past the central coast near Cape Mudge as they weren't bringing many furs but seemed to be bringing trouble by contributing to the trade in vice.[1] The language used was vitriolic and unbridled with racist intolerance that today would be recognized as hate literature. The traders were accused of committing every sort of crime and spreading terror with violence all along the coast until their arrival in Victoria where they "rendered the whole outskirts of the town a perfect brothel." Hateful intolerance was rampant right from the beginning of the establishment of Fort Victoria; the despicable characterization and language used by established leaders was deemed acceptable, and so it would continue. Unsurprisingly, there were indicators that sexual commerce was well established from the earliest times and already controversial.

Opportunities for trade were not limited to local Indigenous groups or the male population. Both men and women came to Fort Victoria with items to sell, such as dried berries, clams, and beans, and they also sought employment as labourers, servants, and guides. As traders and later colonizers arrived in increasing numbers and set up shop, basic needs quickly became apparent—transportation, shelter, food, alcohol, and sex. Not necessarily in that order.

The Hudson's Bay Company had a male workforce, and interaction with Indigenous peoples was largely for trade. The construction of the fort brought local people into closer contact, and the Indigenous peoples' knowledge, expertise, and ability to gather needed items from the land was a definite asset. In addition, the fort was constructed on traditional territory. The local population was later supplemented by workers, known as "Kanaka," brought from the Sandwich Islands (today the Hawaiian Islands) or directly from other HBC forts where they were already employed. Although the local population mainly lived across the harbour, those that stayed in town were segregated along the waterfront and with the Sandwich Islanders in rude shacks on the mud flats in an area called Kanaka Row. In time this became Humboldt Street, and the mud flats and access to the HBC farms was accomplished by a bridge. The flats were filled in 1907–08 to provide the site for the gracious and much-admired Empress Hotel that still overlooks the harbour.

In 1857 Douglas began receiving reports, from HBC mainland chief factors, of the discovery of gold deposits. This was good news, but in the short term it was necessary to keep their own workers in place and not running off to make their perceived fortunes. It was imperative that the HBC move quickly to secure control and keep the new community developing with businesses that supplied goods and services. These grew in sophistication, and sexual commerce was no exception. In the beginning Indigenous inhabitants socialized, traded, and intermingled with the newcomers. Some of the women were in "country marriages," what we would today call common-law, but others were more transient or resided in small huts and shacks along the waterfront.

As to be expected, these arrangements quickly grew to be nuisances to religious members of the community who denounced this flagrant intermingling. The newspapers attempted to paint these women as degraded evil beings, and at best victims, but the community at large took a blind eye to what was considered a necessity; it was left to the clerics and politicians to attempt some condemnation—or at the very least regulation.

In the end, though, one particularly early and noteworthy case was brought by an Indigenous woman known as Kateka and supported by her Kanaka husband Karahue Toimoro. Karahue was taken to jail by local policeman John Westrop Carey, who had returned from prospecting on the Fraser River and taken on the position. The accusation was a count of illegally selling liquor to Indigenous people. The complaint brought by Kateka was that Carey immediately returned to force himself on her, promising he would remove the charges against her husband if she co-operated. Kateka refused and fought back as was witnessed by other women who had gathered to watch through the window and saw Carey becoming increasingly violent. Kateka was saved from rape and immediately sought counsel from two other Kanaka men, Na-hor and William Burns, on how to write to the authorities. They assisted her in getting a letter to Police Magistrate Augustus Pemberton, who had been appointed in 1858.

A CHARGE OF ATTEMPTED RAPE.—Sergt. Joseph W. Carey, of the police force, yesterday appeared before Judge Pemberton, to answer a charge of attempted rape, preferred by a squaw, named Kateka, the wife of a Kanaka, named Karahue. It is charged that about two weeks ago, Carey arrested Karahue on a charge of selling whisky to the Indians; that after he had locked him up, the officer returned and wished to cohabit with the squaw, saying that he would set Karahue free, if she consented; that she refused, and was then thrown down by Carey, who attempted to accomplish his design by force; some other squaws approaching, Carey desisted, and finally went off. Carey states, in defence, that the whole charge is the result of a conspiracy, in which a certain ex-policeman and two members of the force are implicated, and promises to show up the whole affair. Judge Pemberton sent the case to the Assizes, and held Carey to answer in the sum of £40.

British Colonist, July 31, 1860, p. 2

The Grand Jury trial brought several witnesses to court. Carey's defense was that there was a conspiracy over his arrests for selling liquor to "Indians" and that he was hated for disrupting this trade, and so he was being framed. He finished in a summation to the jury, asking them to determine whether they believed the testimony of the witnesses. The eventual outcome of acquittal came as no surprise—after all, the witnesses were women and Indigenous. After a brief (one-minute) consultation, the jurors, who did not get up from their chairs, returned a resounding "not guilty," and it was reported that "the spectators . . . fairly shook the building with their applause." Congratulations and slaps on the back were proffered to Carey, "who was much affected."[2]

As for the women, they were not intimidated by this authority and sought justice through the only means they knew within the colony. Unfortunately, their confidence in the integrity of the authorities proved to be unfounded.

One person who may have wondered about truth in testimony was Pemberton himself, who a year later dispensed with Carey's services as a police sergeant for, in his

Joseph Westrop Carey, disgraced policeman, property owner, landlord to brothel keepers, and mayor of Victoria. *Victoria City Archives M07423*

words, "tippling, insolence to a Police Commissioner [himself], and erasure"[3] alluding to the altering of police charge books by erasing charges, rather than putting a line through so the information was still retained. Carey took himself back to the Fraser River gold fields, but it would not be the last time his presence in the colony would be felt. His popularity among the men in the community served him well in future years when he returned to Victoria and served as a city councillor and alderman between 1869 and 1871. In January 1884 he was elected as mayor, but his tenure in the position was limited to one term.[4]

One of the men who helped Kateka was Na-Hor, who resided on Kanaka Row with an extended family. He had dealt with Carey before when he had been arrested for running a "house of ill-fame." In the legal context of the times, this specifically referred to a place where prostitution was taking place. Terms such as disorderly house, brothel, bawdy house, and house of ill-fame were used interchangeably, all with the same meaning.

There were numerous other places for prostitution besides Kanaka Row. Cabins along what is now Store Street were also characterized as "hotbeds of vice and pollution."[5] Na-Hor was not the first offender to be identified. On July 25, 1858, Christian Callendine, a local worker, was arrested by the sheriff for keeping a "disorderly house," but the charge was dismissed as the evidence was incomplete.[6] Na-Hor wasn't as fortunate, despite his employer, a white man named Samuel Ringo, a restaurant keeper, testifying on his behalf. He was accused of harbouring five or six "half-breed" women, "Indian" women, "half-breed" boys, and Kanakas, all drunk and disorderly with occasional knifings and fights. (Being of mixed blood or "half-breed" was equated with a loss of status and an identifier as an inferior in both settler and Indigenous societies.) For this he served a couple of weeks in jail.[7]

A BROTHEL.—A Kanaka, named Nahor, residing on Humboldt street, was arrested on Sunday by Sergt. Carey, on a charge of keeping a house of ill-fame on Humboldt street, nearly opposite the parsonage grounds. The evidence was pretty strong, and the Police Judge sent the case up to the Court of Sessions.

British Colonist, May 29, 1860, p. 1

Until 1858 policing in Victoria was conducted by a volunteer group largely made up of Metis workers appointed by Chief Factor James Douglas; this group was called the Victoria Voltigeurs, a term taken from French military units. They were responsible for keeping a modicum of civility among the fledgling population. Soon a constable was hired, but by 1858 the aforementioned Augustus Frederick Pemberton, uncle of Joseph Despard Pemberton, colonial surveyor, had arrived to oversee the farmland owned by his nephew. Both were members of an elite Irish family connected to the Lord Mayor of Dublin, and Augustus soon found himself enlisted to establish a police service based on the British system. He was appointed as stipendiary magistrate or justice of the peace, and as chief commissioner of police.

Most crime was of the "disorderly" sort, an all-purpose term that seemed to describe behaviour stemming from the consumption of vast amounts of alcohol. The moralist attitudes of the past combined with a lack of understanding of the cultural and societal differences of the First Nations laid much of the blame for disorderly behaviour on the lower classes of white workers, Indigenous people, and those of mixed ethnicities. Newspapers were full of outrage and judgement by those who felt a moral superiority over those they condemned. Religious leaders, newly arrived, took this movement to a more formalized state and orchestrated protests and court proceedings. Among the earliest were the Wesleyan Methodists.

In the *British Colonist* Reverend Ephraim Evans, a Methodist minister of "high ideals", railed against "crowds of depraved women . . . harboured in the dance houses . . . and then turned out to roam at large in their drunken excitement . . . the whole system of permitting them to frequent the town, or to live in its vicinity, is radically wrong."[8]

Reverend Evans sought to fight what he characterized as "places contributing to the widespread destruction of health, morality and public order" by initiating complaints against Charles King and Christopher Solburgh, who were charged with keeping a disorderly house in the guise of a dance house. The premises were located on Johnson Street between Government and Broad. Reverend Evans spoke of disgustingly lewd language and made it clear he disapproved of dancing, let alone more intimate connections. Neighbours backed him up. David Hart complained of profane and obscene language.

> *I am in the habit of passing the said building every night and on each night of the past week . . . a number of disorderly persons have been congregated in front of the said building, and on the Public footpath using profane & obscene language . . . the noise arising from the music, dancing and shouting is intolerable.*[9]

Rev. Ephraim Evans, D.D., served as grand superintendent of the British Columbia Missions for nine years. *Canadian Methodist Historical Society (Rootsweb)*

John Mendoza testified to seeing couples with arms around each other's necks, "stamping and dancing and hollering and hooting" and added he was distressed to see "numbers of little Indian girls with white men . . . using very indecent language."

The owners of the building, Thomas Patrick and James Reid Robertson, stated there had been no complaints of excessive noise or obscene language. The bartender and proprietors of the adjoining hotel and bars had no complaints. Most importantly, neither did the police. James Reid McAdams, a police officer, testified it was no worse than usual and that it closed at midnight, although others claimed 1:00 or 2:00 AM was more common. He knew the "Indian women" made their living by prostitution, but another police officer, Metcalfe, offered a different perspective, saying he knew the women lived with the men as housekeepers. Police Sergeant Arthur McBride concluded nothing immoral was going on, and they all agreed David Hart's language was as "disorderly and rough" as anyone's. It was a case that went nowhere.[10]

Despite much controversy in the 1860s, dance houses—or the more offensive "squaw houses," a demeaning, racist label—remained popular, and authorities tended to look away. For the number of men passing through Victoria to and from the gold fields they were a primary destination for relaxation and a place to spend their newfound fortunes, particularly for those who were not likely to be invited to the dances of the town's elite. A description of a miner's dance hall in the Cariboo exists and gives some colour to what can only be imagined from this distance.

> *. . . 25 [cents] was the entrance fee and there was a kind of Master of the Ceremonies, who called out the figures saying, "first gent to the left, with the left hand round, back again and turn, balance in line" . . . it was really wonderful what good time they all kept, and how serious they all were about it. All the girls were either Kitty or Polly . . . and when the quadrille was finished, "Waltz up to the bar" was shouted out in a very loud voice.*[11]

The dance houses soon had their day as far as places of assignation for sexual commerce, and the more comfortable hotels, lodging houses, and even theatres became popular choices. One early purveyor in this transition was Henrietta Immel, formerly of San Francisco, and her eventual spouse, the well-named William Lush. In 1862 Henrietta operated the Metropolitan Lodging House, but she faced a charge of allowing prostitution to be carried on in her premises. The charge was eventually dropped, and she joined with Lush—who himself ran a couple of saloons—in matrimony and business. They constructed a hotel outside the populated area of Victoria and near to the racecourse at Beacon Hill Park. The well-known Park Hotel enjoyed a lively and varied clientele over the years. Henrietta continued to make trips to San Francisco, as was revealed in published passenger lists, and occasionally came back accompanied by women to "work" in the hotel in ways that were viewed with suspicion.

Theatres had offerings much like those found in dance houses. Some theatre performances were held in saloons or hotels, but by 1860 the first theatre premises, rudimentary though they were, opened. In the late 1850s to mid-1860s, there was theatre for the elite, and there was theatre for the entertainment of the others—predominantly the miners. And it was a convenient place to meet and mingle with members of the opposite sex.

Music halls predated the legitimate theatre. They were run as an offshoot of the music and dance rooms attached to saloons—almost a cross between a dance house and a proper theatre. They had a stage and gallery or box seats where attractive young women interacted with customers according to how much they were willing to pay. On the menu was everything from drinking and playful flirtation to full sexual activity. Unlike at the proper theatres, muddy boots, dirty clothes, raucous and leering laughter, and whisky breath were acceptable. In time the two types of theatres began to combine, with segregated areas for the prostitutes who would make arrangements for customers to come to the brothels. For this reason theatres retained a slightly immoral impression in some minds. Actresses were looked upon as occupying a middle ground of morality, dependent on their choice and execution of theatrical performance. For one socially prominent family from the fur trade days, the idea that a family member might follow this path was abhorrent. In a letter written in 1870, Dr. William Fraser Tolmie, HBC surgeon and fur trader, tried to dissuade his twenty-year-old son Alexander from falling prey to the "wretched life of a player" in the theatrical world.

> *When it was mentioned to him that about theatres he would be exposed to the evil example of dissipated associates he at once of his own accord joined the Good Templars . . . His mother and I have done our best to induce him to abandon this craving after the Stage, so we have given up.*[12]

Theatrical troupes moved from venue to venue, many originating in San Francisco and through the developing towns northward. Their repertoire consisted of musical entertainments and short plays. One of these groups was led by a man named Richard Cranshaw, an actor from New York. Cranshaw, also a noted playwright, was well known along the coast for his acting abilities and for the calibre of players who accompanied him. One was his lover, Nettie Sager.

BENEFIT OF MR. CRANSHAW.—Mr. Bell's theatrical company will this evening recommence performances in this city with a benefit to Mr. Richard Cranshaw, on which occasion "Ireland as it was," "The Queen's Own," and several ballads will be given. The company comprises many of Victoria's greatest favorites, among whom are Messrs. Beatty, Thayer, Cranshaw and Potter, and Misses Dean and Howard. Miss Netty Sager will make her *debut* in this place to-night. Mr. Cranshaw is a good *artiste* and a worthy man, and deserves a full house.

British Colonist, October 13, 1862, p. 2

— *Nettie's Story* —

Nettie Sager (AKA *Rosalie Cooper*)

NETTIE SAGER MADE HER FIRST APPEARANCE ON A VICTORIA STAGE in 1862, and it is here we pick up her story. Although there is little primary information on her, even anything to determine her real name, her honesty and strong personality come through in court records and newspaper reports; while researching her, I was drawn to her story by her seemingly cheerful acceptance of her life choices. Like her theatrical performances, her life, eventful and even entertaining, reveals a collection of emotions, titillation, and pathos. Time, distance, and perhaps a whole lot of secrecy may keep her full life hidden from view, but even these abbreviated revelations show the kinds of attitudes in a colonial town experiencing rapid growth and change.

Newspapers provide a glimpse into the world Nettie inhabited with friends, like the unhappily married Emma Jane Pringle and the newly arrived Martha Goodwin, fresh off the boat as a seeker of domestic work in the new colony. These women, including Nettie, were eventually employed by saloon keeper Lewis Davis, who, much to his embarrassment, found his Star & Garter saloon featured prominently as the setting for Nettie's most dramatic episode. He may well have rued the day he let her through the door. But the tale begins with Richard Cranshaw, Nettie's lover, theatrical mentor, and intermittent abuser.

According to Nettie, she arrived in Victoria with Richard Cranshaw after she was widowed in February 1862. As part of a theatre company, she played parts in several farcical and musical performances and then decided to become an entrepreneur. In April 1863 she opened the Bouquet Baths and Refreshment Saloon adjacent to the Colonial Hotel on Government Street and advertised catering for comfort, cleanliness, fine food, and cigars.

Later, in testimony before the courts, she said that she had been an actress, barkeeper, seamstress, and anything else one could think of: "I never refused anything that was offered to me."[13] This saloon business was short-lived, and Nettie's sojourn in the night life of Victoria did not go unnoticed. Her choices—even her cigar smoking—would come back to haunt her.

Much more would be revealed in police court when Lewis Davis, proprietor of the Star & Garter, was charged for allowing a notorious woman (i.e., Nettie Sager) to work there. It appears this was against licensing regulations, although Davis's solicitor Robert Bishop argued this point. In addition, Bishop took issue with Augustus Frederick Pemberton as a stipendiary magistrate exceeding his powers in passing judgement on Davis's case.

Actor and playwright Richard Cranshaw (AKA Donovan) had been charged for the attempted knifing of Lewis Davis—with a motive that mainly revolved around Nettie. At that court case, Pemberton

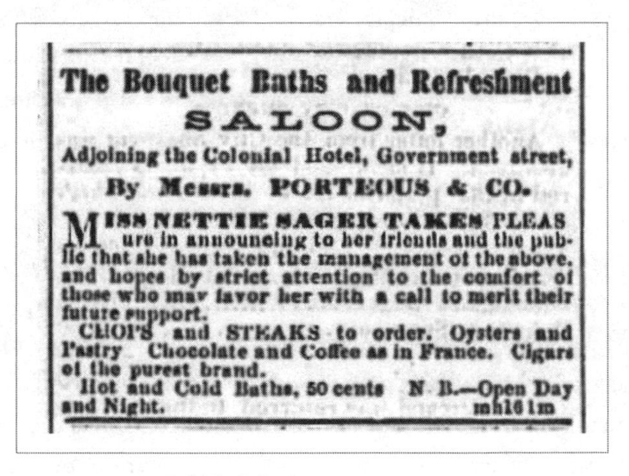

British Colonist, May 11, 1863, p. 3

already knew of the trials and tribulations of Nettie and Cranshaw's relationship: They had appeared before him in June of 1863 when Cranshaw had, according to the newspaper, "violently assaulted and threatened the life" of Rosalie Cooper (one of Nettie's aliases from her travels along the coast). The evidence provided by witnesses showed what Pemberton already knew to be a pattern with this couple: When drunk, Cranshaw was prone to attacking Nettie physically and holding her against her will. During the incident in question, she climbed out a window, as observed by two bystanders who came to her aid. In that June court appearance, Pemberton ordered Cranshaw to pay a fine and keep the peace for three months. He did so, but for the next two months Cranshaw constantly dogged Nettie's heels, drunk, depressed, and desperately professing his love. He continued to try to see her and showed up at dances and to the Star & Garter saloon. According to Lewis Davis, this included bursting through the door "like a maniac" and running around the billiard tables. Davis questioned Cranshaw's sanity and told Nettie that her continued employment depended on not seeing Cranshaw.

Nettie now made seventy-five dollars a month and was given a private room. She was responsible for all her own expenses, including meals. She and Martha, her fellow employee at the Star & Garter, managed to find companions willing to treat them at Jacobi's restaurant nearby. Emma Jane Pringle, another waitress, was in a war of advertisements with her estranged husband, a mariner by the name of Edwin H. Pringle. She was placing prominent ads in the *Colonist* declaring that he was not giving her any money and that she was "forced to appear nightly at the Star & Garter." He responded with an even larger ad that he certainly was supporting her. In the end he arrived at the Star & Garter and took her home. Nettie's reputation and Emma Pringle's very public marriage difficulties worked together to cast suspicion on the activities at the Star & Garter.

When all of this was revealed in court testimony, Lewis Davis attempted to paint a picture of himself as an employer who kept things under tight control. The women were not allowed visitors upstairs, he said, adding that he had a wife himself. He did admit to occasionally sleeping at the saloon and that he rented to other lodgers occasionally. The women were expected to come down to the saloon and behave respectably, getting drink orders and then retiring to their rooms at 11:00 PM or 1:00 AM, 2:00 AM at the latest. Other witnesses pointed out that Lewis was known to hire "pretty waiter girls." After hearing all of this, Pemberton reiterated his strong feelings that there were matters of importance that must be explored to strike at the "root of evil."

Other witness testimony told of Cranshaw showing up at the Star & Garter, as he did regularly over the preceding few weeks, brandishing a Bowie knife, a relic of the civil war. He insisted on seeing Nettie in her room, and despite the best efforts of the bar staff he made his way there. He waved his knife at Lewis, who was sitting with Nettie in her room, but it was Nettie and her friend Martha who disarmed him with a headlock and a sharp jerk backwards that sent the knife out of his reach. This testimony was provided by Martha herself, who proclaimed it with much pride.

Cranshaw decided to throw himself on the mercy of the court, using his best theatrical devices to plead his case:

> *I know I have done wrong, very wrong; in fact I have been insane, but I have always objected to Miss Sager going to . . . nothing else but an assignation house.*
>
> *I love that woman; this is no jesting matter . . . I did my best to make a good girl of her, but he* [Lewis] *has been working against me. I know I stand in a frightful situation; my character is gone. I have a mother at New York, 70 years of age, and what will she say? If possible, let me leave the colony and never see the woman again.*[14]

According to Nettie, she had been married up until a few months before the court case but was now a widow. She had taken up with Cranshaw and was part of his theatrical troupe, as was borne out by the many advertisements for their productions at the Victoria Theatre. She had been living with him at the Colonial Hotel but found his violent jealously not in keeping with her free-thinking approach to life. She even confessed she herself had to lock Cranshaw up a few times during his fits of insanity.

Despite Davis's instructions to stay away from Cranshaw, she admitted she did spend time with him, going for walks and even agreeing to dance with him at the Star & Garter one night. It went surprisingly well, according to Nettie. Cranshaw sang and played the piano and left in an orderly manner. She testified her dance partners included a man named Edgecombe, who was keeping company with Martha Goodwin, and a "crazy" blacksmith whose name she couldn't remember. Oh yes—and then there was Eugene, the cook from the St. Nicholas Hotel. Nettie's sense of innocence and her theatrical delivery when recounting the men she knew caused no end of amusement, and by this time laughter was rolling through the courtroom.

As the testimony proceeded it was shown that the next day was quite different: another demand for entry, a hidden knife, and a scuffle with Ebney, a staff member who got possession of the weapon by biting Cranshaw's fingers. In the end, though, Nettie made a heartfelt testimony that she had seen Cranshaw overworked and emotional in the theatre in a way that she believed showed temporary insanity—but she concluded "when these fits are not upon him he is one of the best men I ever knew." Robert Bishop, the defense attorney, praised her for her fair evidence and devotion shown to the prisoner.

As the case continued in subsequent days it quickly became two cases: the original against Cranshaw, and a new one against Lewis Davis. Pemberton summoned Davis on breaching the licensing rules by wilfully permitting Nettie Sager, a notoriously bad character (as Pemberton had described her), to frequent his house. Davis had terminated her employment a few days earlier, perhaps in fear of this turn of events. Robert Bishop, now counsel to both Cranshaw and Davis, objected strenuously to trying the two cases together:

> *Mr. Bishop said that such a mode of procedure was unheard of and contrary to the principles of English Law, as while a charge was being heard against one man to call him into the witness box to give evidence in a charge against another man.*

To this, Pemberton responded,

> *In that case I will dismiss the charge against Cranshaw.*[15]

Bishop then threw every objection he could about Pemberton's authority to try a licensing case, but Pemberton sidestepped each objection. Undoubtedly frustrated with Bishop's constant challenges, Pemberton granted only enough time for Davis to produce his licence. Pemberton admitted he could not cancel the licence but believed he could try an infraction on breach of good order. He was determined in his belief that "this was a question that affected the morality of the town and was one of great importance to the community."[16]

Officer Wilmer testified visiting the Star & Garter just after midnight on Sunday, July 26, when a large group of people were in attendance. He thought them respectable except for Nettie, whom he knew had been an inmate of a house of ill-fame:

> *I cannot swear that Nettie Sager was not a seamstress in the house of ill-fame. I am not aware that seamstresses work in those houses. It was about 8 or 9 o'clock at night about five or six weeks ago, I saw her leave the house. I know that many men live with Indian women but I don't know about white women. I have seen her in Government and Yates Street at an early hour in the morning when modest women would not be walking about.*
>
> *[To the bench] I never saw her smoke but heard she does.*
>
> *[Mr. Bishop] Oh, I object to that; some of the officials' wives here smoke. [Laughter]*
>
> *[Officer Abson] Had seen the girl about 2 or 3 o'clock in the morning, coming from Jacobi's with a cigar in her mouth.*[17]

The case continued with more testimony from Cranshaw. Martha and numerous patrons and neighbours of the Star & Garter all painted the establishment as respectable—save Cranshaw who was suspicious of the place and Nettie's activities. Bishop continued to invoke laughter with remarks about Martha and Nettie:

> [*Bishop*] *Your Worship forgets that this girl* [*referring to Martha*] *is going to be married . . . and I am informed that Nettie Sager is in the same happy state. Mr. Cranshaw will have to seek another wife.*
>
> [*Cranshaw*] *Mr. Bishop, please jest upon some other subject.*[18]

In the end Pemberton still felt there was reason to believe Davis had compromised his licence by allowing Nettie to work in his establishment. He indicated some sympathy for Davis, who he believed to be of good character, and so fined him the minimum of five pounds for a first offense:

> *It is my desire that the character of hotels should be fully known, that respectable women may have no fear of going to them. When people go to such places as squaw houses or houses of ill-fame, they know what they are doing. I consider that squaw houses do more good than harm, as it collects the Indian women, who would otherwise be loitering about the streets, in one spot where they can be under surveillance of the police. Such a class of house as the present one is, in my opinion, highly dangerous.*

> *It is proved to my satisfaction, and well known to all, that the woman, Nettie Sager, is a "notoriously bad character."*[19]

Emma's husband had taken her away shortly after the court appearance. Nettie and Martha had to seek other employment, and Cranshaw was sent back to the US with help from his friends. In May 1864, a San Francisco newspaper reported that Richard had taken his own life by ingesting laudanum. The story was shared by newspapers all along the west coast, due to his reputation and notoriety. Cranshaw was thirty-two years old when he died.

> *SUICIDE - Richard CRANSHAW took laudanum in San Francisco on Saturday and died yesterday, though the poison was removed from his stomach. He is the actor who, in company with Forbes, another member of a theatrical troupe visiting this city 2 or 3 years ago, attacked Mr. BIVEN . . . CRANSHAW has been frequently before the public in other positions than that of an actor.*[20]

Where Nettie originally came from, and where she ended up, is lost in the historical record, perhaps to be discovered one day. Attempts to track her through published passenger lists, newspaper accounts of theatrical billings, directories, vital statistics records, or death notices under the names of Nettie Sager (a nickname for many common names such as Henrietta, Annette, and even Helen) or Rosalie Cooper have not yielded much. Furthermore, her familiarity with many towns along the west coast makes her moves daunting to follow. She undoubtedly left the colony after being so publicly branded as an undesirable character. As an actress and transitory figure, it was easy to take a new name, a new lover, or even a new husband and move on to the next developing town along the coast; these were times when anonymity was easily found and a fresh start was assured.

Along with fortune seekers came the opportunists, some legitimate and some after a quick con. Women like Nettie might find stability with a partner or even marriage, but they were always ready to move on if conditions made that necessary, particularly for one who boasted of never declining an opportunity. Her attempts at running her own business had been short-lived: She closed her saloon after a few months in business—perhaps after leaving Cranshaw, who lived in the adjacent hotel—but her tenacity might have served her better in another place. Her few years in Victoria leave us with an impression of a strong and perhaps reckless spirit who is part of the history of the place.

—

With a transitory population of gold seekers came many nationalities, particularly coming via California where the goldfields were losing their productiveness. From the very beginning it was a multiracial and multicultural community and still predominantly male. The rapid increase in the size and complexity of the population made for constant adjustments—but one thing was for certain: there would always be men seeking the comforts of female company.

Chapter Two

CAPITAL, CONFEDERATION, AND "COMPANY LADIES"

THE 1870S WAS A DECADE OF ESTABLISHMENT. IN 1862, THE colony of Vancouver Island rapidly transformed from an HBC outpost to an island colony. In 1866, the colony united with the mainland—and then in 1871, there was Confederation. While Victoria was the capital of the island colony and New Westminster the capital of the mainland colony, a campaign and vote was undertaken to determine which should be the capital of the united colony and subsequently the newly created province. After much heated debate, Victoria elbowed aside the pretender and proudly revealed herself as the capital, to be forever associated with the indomitable British queen, Victoria. Like Queen Victoria, the town was solid, well established, and full of energy and vision.

Frame buildings like the saloon and dance hall Star & Garter were replaced with brick, and several new and substantial buildings dotted the streets, making the crude shacks on the waterfront even more of an eyesore. The fort had for the most part been dismantled in the late 1840s, and the buildings erected in haste (to deal with the influx of miners heading to and from the goldfields in the late 1850s and early '60s) were no longer adequate. The town took on a new aspect, now being part of the Dominion of Canada, with political agendas gaining more importance in building a vital city—and land ownership even more so.

One problem area was the rapidly expanding Chinatown. In practical ways it had become a law unto itself with its own powerful society, or tong—the Chi Kung Tong acting in most aspects of life, even criminal matters. The Chi Kung Tong was a part of the Triad Society, in turn descended from the Hung League who were largely a secret society and politically motivated to make changes in China.[1] They had control and power over their citizens, even overseas. The predominantly male population was guided by the political and social leadership of the Tong and in turn maintained their loyalty. Most men, like their non-Chinese counterparts, set off for the goldfields, while some stayed to provide supplies and services such as laundry, cooking, market gardening, and the sourcing of materials important to their culture, both ceremonial and religious.

The Chi Kung Tong was first established in British Columbia having expanded from the San Francisco area and the mining towns of California into the goldfields—but it also maintained a presence in Victoria, which became increasingly active in the late nineteenth and early twentieth centuries. However, even in the 1860s and '70s they influenced the newly forming Chinatown, with property ownership, opium factories (which were legal), and the importation of women to serve as prostitutes.[2]

Part of the agreement around British Columbia joining Confederation was the building of the Canadian Pacific Railway (CPR). This necessitated a large workforce, and accordingly an estimated 16,000 workers were brought from China to fulfill this need; upon completion in 1885 the workers settled into existing Chinatowns, particularly in Vancouver and Victoria.[3]

But before Chinatown got to this stage it was already viewed by the non-Chinese community as a problem. The *British Colonist* in

Victoria's Chinatown developed quickly from a collection of shacks to a more sophisticated aspect, still with a predominantly male population. *Courtesy of the author*

May of 1876 reported that nine brothels were operating there. As these prostitutes were not servicing only the residents of Chinatown, the question was raised by City Councillor Noah Shakespeare about what action could be taken to shut down the brothels. Council, "while admitting of the extreme and grave character of the evil" in the immediate period had done nothing as it was considered "a very difficult subject to deal with."[4]

In June City Council was still trying to shut them down. As with the Indigenous people, here was another instance of societies with their own traditions, beliefs, and societal norms clashing with the religious and moral attitudes of a powerful segment of the dominating culture. The Chinese miners' and workers' experiences in California had taught them they would not be served well in a

CHINESE BROTHELS.—It has been ascertained that Chinese women are in the habit of luring boys of tender age into their dens after dark, and several fine, promising lads have been ruined for life in consequence. The Police are about to make a descent on the horrid holes with the view to their suppression. We believe, also, that a new Police regulation is about to be instituted with respect to boys who, when caught on the streets after nightfall, will be taken to the barracks for safekeeping.

British Colonist, June 14, 1876, p. 2

system rife with racism and corruption. They may have been skeptical of these seemingly altruistic efforts, and suspected them of being attached to the auspices of the various churches. But in time, leaders in their own community would join forces to assist women and children in difficult situations, with varying degrees of success.

Violent occurrences were the extent of police intervention. In late June it was Inspector Bowden who attended to complaints of a woman screaming in a building adjacent to Duck's carriage factory on the corner of Broad and Johnson Streets. He pushed into the room and found the woman, Ah Quay, lying on a bed and a man, later identified as Ah Lun, attempting to make an escape. Both appeared in court, and the inspector testified that Ah Quay was "known as a common prostitute" who solicited customers by sitting in the window. The judge ruled there was no evidence that Ah Lun was a frequenter, and he discharged him—adding that he could testify against the woman. A week before, Mariano Cruz was arrested for causing a disturbance in a Chinese brothel over the price of two dollars. Cruz fought with the woman, took possession of her clothes, and attempted to flee when he was apprehended. The judge dismissed the case, stating that the disturbance occurred indoors, and he was not inclined "to afford the inmates of such places any assistance in carrying on their nefarious traffic."[5]

For the ambitious developer, buying up lots in the central area was a prudent move. One who moved in quickly to secure prime land was Louis (or Ludwig) Vigelius, a German immigrant who arrived in Victoria by way of San Francisco and established a hairdressing business about 1867. He had been in business with two other German immigrant barbers in San Francisco and likely learned his trade with them. In Victoria he took a partner, John Becker, and established the St. Nicholas Hair Saloon (*saloon* and *salon* were interchangeable terms at this time) on Government Street. In a few years Becker was gone, and Louis's brothers Anton and John joined the business. Louis married a woman named Maria Castro and wasted no time in immersing himself in local politics, spending several years as a city councillor. He had energy, opinions, and a decided lack of scruples as he joined in the cries to clean up the brothels in Chinatown and peripheral areas. And yet he chose not to worry too much about his own properties and the money that flowed in from renting them out to brothel keepers.[6]

One of the prime areas for property ownership was right in the middle of town on Broad Street, which already housed a few basic transitory brothel operations. Ludwig Vigelius owned property here, as did Simeon Duck, a local businessman who operated a carriage and wagon factory and later become active in provincial politics. On December 14, 1876, Duck served on a grand in which the opening statements from Justice Crease emphasized rather pointedly that "they should be cognisant of social evils such as brothels and to indict those connected with them."[7]

The following day the grand jury presented a report on the sanitary conditions of the city with respect to dance halls and brothels and the growing fear of the spread of smallpox. They never did seem to get to the root of the role and responsibility the ownership of properties played, and focused their efforts on sanitation. The dance halls were closed, and trade moved to the centre of town. Chinatown, along with Broughton, Broad, Johnson, and Cormorant Streets—with small brothel operations, saloons, and theatres—became the new area for sexual assignations. Having solved the immediate problem of dance houses and sanitation, the jury suggested they could now be disbanded.

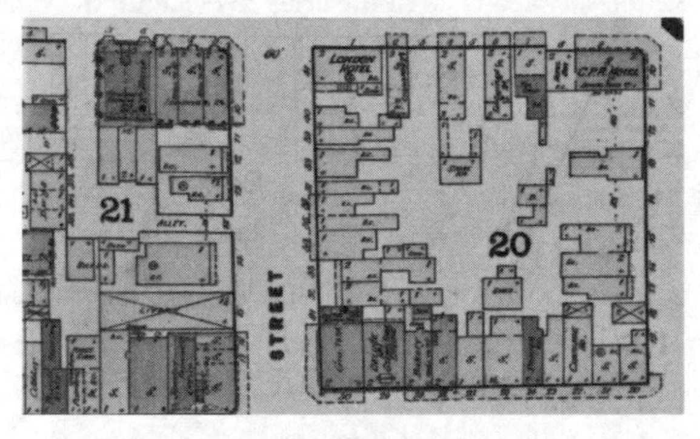

A portion of the Sanborn Fire Insurance Map of Victoria in 1885 showing a block of Broad Street with a row of small houses including the one where Martha Gillespie lived. *Library of Congress, Map and Geography Division*

— *Martha's Story* —

(AKA *Gillespie, Smith, Haley, Bolduc, Dalbery*)

As I approached Martha's story, I was struck by how much it seemed to be one of chaos. Within a few short years she seemed to marry a couple of times in the Methodist Church a block away from her brothel residence on Broad Street, without benefit of divorce. All was dutifully recorded in legal documents to be found in Vital Statistics' records. As I delved deeper into her story, having discerned what her maiden name was (Gillespie) and what her origins were by tracing her genealogy, I caught a glimpse of a life that was adventurous, tragic, and ill-planned, perhaps indicating what might have been a mental illness, alcohol dependence, or just plain recklessness. Coming from a rural background and an early marriage, she seemed to chart her life by learning the hard way.

Martha Gillespie spent her childhood on her parents' small pig farm in Iowa, where her father Andrew supplemented the family income with bronco-busting and hunting deer and buffalo. She was the sixth out of thirteen children born to Temperance (Bankston) Gillespie. She was still living at home in the 1850s, and in the 1860 US census she is recorded as Martha Smith "servant" with a two-year-old daughter, Sophia, and a six-month-old baby boy, Alfred William. She was married at the age of sixteen to an Englishman from a nearby farm, William Smith. Smith and his brothers, Philip and Alfred Wellington, were intrigued by the tales of goldfields in a place called British Columbia; as life was a struggle on the farms of the Midwest, Philip and Alfred set off to explore the possibilities.

A short time later William and Martha followed, after the tragic death of young Sophia in March of 1861. For Martha, with a toddler to care for, it was a particularly daunting journey, but it was one filled with hopes for a more promising future. When they arrived in the colony of mainland British Columbia they went straight for the town of Lillooet, where Alfred began in partnership as a general merchant with his sister Sophia and her husband Franklin Eastman. They met with some success, and Alfred stayed in the area for several decades. He served as a member of the Legislative Assembly from 1889 to 1903. Philip lived in Douglas, BC, and was a merchant and transportation entrepreneur. He married Sylvestria Layzell; they had four boys but endured a difficult family life and setbacks in business.[8]

William and Martha's route is not so clear; they were both in Victoria by the early 1870s but living separately. Young Alfred may have resided with his father, whose health was declining, but as the years passed he followed his own path to the Okanagan where he married fifteen-year-old Susan Jane McNeill. With her father and brother, Alfred established himself as a stock raiser in the Vernon area. He spent the rest of his life there.

Despite the fact that William was still living, and that there is no record of a divorce, Martha married in October of 1875, giving all the correct information except for calling herself a spinster. The groom was a local Quebec-born blacksmith, Joseph Bolduc, age thirty-three.[9]

Whether married or a bigamist, Martha began appearing in police records for offenses, including prostitution, under the names Martha Smith, Healy, or Haley. She lived on Broad Street right in the middle of the developing town surrounded by a mix of businesses, saloons, homes, shanties, and a Chinese laundry. Directly adjacent to her premises were the London Hotel; a prominent physician, Dr. Trimble; and the appropriately named James Moss, florist. Other shanties housed one to three sex workers, including the madam. They all identified themselves as dressmakers, a common euphemism used for official records. Court registers, police documents, and newspapers told the real story, sometimes in lurid detail. Number 5 Broad Street was the home and operating premises for Martha's sole-proprietor business.

As I discovered, she did have help on occasion. On a chilly November evening in 1876, Inspector Bowden was taking a stroll down Broad Street when the door to No. 5 opened and a man looked out. Bowden knew this was a house of bad character and immediately questioned the man. He gave his name as John Cameron, and after throwing out a few vitriolic words at the officer admitted he was the "doorkeeper." Bowden later testified he had never known him to do anything but "capping" for houses of prostitution—an old English term for pimping.[10] Bowden hauled Cameron off to jail, and he was charged with vagrancy, the oft-used charge for habitués of brothels.

The following Tuesday at police court—possibly still stinging from the insulting language Cameron had abused him with—the inspector went on to illustrate the dangers of the local brothels; he testified that he was told of problems experienced by returning miners and surveyors from the Cassiar district who, while on a spree, were enticed into one of the Broad Street houses and robbed of their money.

Then it was Martha's (or Mary Haley, as she was now calling herself) turn to provide an explanation for her house guest. She stated John had returned from California six weeks earlier and found employment, lost it, and had then come to work for her as a nurse, as she had been unwell. He had been known to do this for another woman.

His Honour H.C. Courtney was not buying it and proceeded to let Cameron know what he thought of him and his ilk.

> [*I*] *could not imagine a more degraded thing than a young man, strong and heathy . . . living on the prostitution of dissolute women. It was disgraceful that honest men who toiled all*

> *summer in the mines earning their money by the sweat of their brow . . . should be pounced on or "corralled" . . . by one of these blackguards—pimps for these houses.*[11]

He finished with a final shot at Martha, noting if she really wanted a nurse, she would have hired a girl. A sentence of one month with hard labour and a fifty-dollar fine was imposed on Cameron, who was lucky he escaped the maximum six-month sentence.

Martha went on to become a well-known participant in police court with charges of stealing and the use of loud and obscene language in the streets. She was obviously not one to move on quickly, either: The residents of the shanties changed quickly, but the one constant was Martha in the middle, with no inclination to leave.[12]

Mrs. Dolbery, charged with unlawfully creating a disturbance and using abusive language on Broad street on the 14th day of June last, was fined $10 or 14 days' imprisonment.

James Russell, charged with being in the habit of frequenting a house of ill-fame situate on Broad street, and also annoying the neighbors in that locality and with having no visible means of support except living on the prostitution of certain women in the said locality, that this day, June 14th, he was out with nothing but his shirt and pants on his person, and was unlawfully making a disturbance at a house of ill-fame in the street aforesaid.

His Honor fined the prisoner $10 or 14 days' imprisonment.

British Colonist, June 16, 1878

Less than a year later, on July 28, 1877, Martha married again—this time calling herself a widow, although no death record has been found for Bolduc, and William was still alive.[13] Her groom this time was Swedish immigrant Karl Mangims Dalbery, a labourer. Records for Dalbery, like Bolduc, are sparse; he doesn't appear to have spent much time in Victoria. Almost a year later Martha had another house guest, James Russell, who with his belligerent behaviour on the streets landed them both back in court.

All the while William, her husband, who had been suffering from illness for years, was living on Johnson Street a short distance away. In 1881 he died of pneumonia, and the census taken in the same year now described Martha as a widow. Despite all the turmoil and recent events, Martha still stayed put. The census recorded her as a dress-maker, age forty, still living next to Dr. Trimble. In 1883 the proximity to a doctor should have been an advantage, but in a rather dramatic turn of events he was no help at all.[14]

Martha's landlord, Robert Anderson of Lochend Farm in Saanich, died in August of 1883. It fell to his son John to break the news to Martha and possibly move her along. This meeting rapidly deteriorated into a spree, with copious amounts of alcohol as the fuel. The pair set off on a wild ride through the town and out past Beacon Hill Park on a rough road. The return trip was not so easy. The buggy flipped on the uneven grading coming down from the park to the James Bay bridge. A couple of sailors came by and helped her get John back to her place. A dazed and drunk Martha made her way to Dr. Trimble's door, but with no reply to her frantic knocking and yelling. She summoned the night watchman, who promptly arrested her and took her to jail. After hearing her rather hysterical account, Constable Hough returned with her. Seeing poor Anderson laid out on the parlour floor, he called for Dr. Jackson, who declared him deceased. The inquest held the following day concluded John had died from injuries that were consistent with a fall from a buggy.[15]

Martha finally disappeared from Victoria around 1884–5, and reliable evidence as to where she went is sparse. The records I looked at, particularly the 1900 US Census for Portland, Oregon, showed a woman who had many similarities. She is recorded as Martha Smith (living with a Harry Smith) who was born in Iowa in 1841, mother of two children who were both deceased. All of this is consistent with information given in Canadian census records by Martha, except that her son was still alive, but she may not have known this.[16]

This Martha and her husband lived between two Chinese laundries at 533 Goldsmith Street, and according to the census they married in 1885. Goldsmith Street in Portland no longer exists but was a rough area with brothels and saloons, close to Chinatown. No death records have emerged to confirm this identity, nor any photographs.

Nebraska's *St. Paul Republican* newspaper in 1905 included a photograph of a family gathering honouring the 100th birthday of Andrew Gillespie.[17] He is surrounded by family and is noted for his upstanding character, having "never chewed or smoked tobacco, drank liquor, or used profane language," and his dedication to his Methodist faith. There is no mention if Martha was among the thousand people said to have attended the celebration.

Gillespie family reunion in Nebraska. Martha's father is in the second-row centre, sixth adult from the left. *St. Paul Republican* newspaper, June 22, 1905, p. 1

Changes continued in the Broad Street area of Victoria. More substantial buildings went up, and although brothels remained, they were a little more upscale and discreet. Prostitution was slightly more businesslike with agreements and chattel mortgages drawn up. Many of these records still survive in land titles offices and government archives. Martha's chaotic and free-living ways would not have fit in well in that environment; that, combined with the death of her landlord's son, and the growing prominence of some of her family members, may have convinced her to leave.

Chapter Three

LANDLORDS, LADIES, AND LOST SOULS

THE 1880S WERE A TIME OF EXPANSION IN BUSINESS FOR SOME companies, particularly those directly involved in service to a growing population. One of these, the Victoria Transfer Company, was ready to take on the future with plans of establishing streetcar lines to supplement their hack (taxi) business, carriage building, storage and rental, stabling for fifty horses with expansion to one hundred, and passenger and luggage transfer from incoming steamers. Their existing premises at Yates and Government were too small, and they purchased land on Broughton Street from the corner of Gordon extending through to Courtney Street. They built a large stable in the middle of this block of Broughton, a carriage works on the corner, and in between a frame house to accommodate an office. On the far side of the stable was another building with a series of small individual rooms intended for workers' residences.

Business opportunities were there, and as both population and land development grew, this extended to the sex industry. Victoria was a well-known and admired up-and-coming community along the coast, and for those wanting to start a business that might not meet with their friends' and family's approval, it offered opportunities to start anonymously. Victoria was a known quantity to other communities along the coast and shared a common economic history fuelled by gold rushes, transportation, trade, and service industries. And if things didn't work out for the entrepreneurs, they could go home—it was an easy journey. Numerous steamers arrived from San Francisco, Seattle, Tacoma, Port Angeles, and Port Townsend and went onward to Vancouver and New Westminster. There was a well-established route through California to Oregon and Washington.

In 1883 one of these steamers arrived from San Francisco with a woman known as Henrietta Morgan and her "lady's companion" Pauline Massoulle. According to Pauline the two had met in Los Angeles where Henrietta, then known as Mrs. O'Connor, had operated a grocery but was robbed by her husband and so wanted to leave town. She persuaded Pauline to go with her to San Francisco and then to carry on to Victoria with Pauline as her companion, in exchange for her passage and twenty dollars a month.[1] When they arrived, Henrietta set about purchasing a property with a house on Broughton Street right next to the Victoria Transfer Company.

Interestingly, she placed an advertisement on the front page of the *Colonist* in July and August 1883 that simply read "Hattie P. Morgan, 321 Sutter Street, San Francisco, California." The advertisement ran for two months, perhaps to establish her previous credentials. Business connections with San Francisco were strong, with many companies having locations in each city. Hattie's advertisement was likely to capitalize on already established ties with many who travelled to each city. At the very least it shows her business savvy.

An empty lot on one side and a stable on the other would give her the privacy her business demanded. It was a two-storey frame house with twelve small rooms. Pauline, at least according to her, was on duty from 7:00 AM to 12:00 noon to prepare breakfast and tend to her employer's large and fine wardrobe as needed. But it appears things did not go well. Pauline left in April of 1885 after Henrietta's health declined and she felt "she could not help her." She endeavoured to recover wages she felt she was owed and even approached lawyer Samuel Perry Mills about acting. He declined, according to Pauline, "for personal reasons of his own." Henrietta continued operating despite her health problems and was identified on a list compiled by Police Chief Charles P. Bloomfield to show the extent of the proprietors and owners of houses of ill-fame in the city as of April 7, 1886.[2]

In his list and accompanying note Charles Bloomfield described the situation in the city. He carefully pointed out in his report to the police committee that although "there are a number of Indian women in the City, prostitutes who have no fixed place of abode," he did not include them as "they are coming and leaving the city at all times." Nor did he include all of the Chinese-owned houses,

April 7 — 1906

List of Houses of ill-fame in the City.

Name of occupier	Locality	Name of Owner	No of Women
Nettie Holt	Broad St.	Mrs Doane	3.
Mable Vaughn	"	" "	4.
Jennie Nelson	"	" "	3.
Louisa	"	" "	3.
Mary Kelly	"	L. Vigelius	2.
Josie Williams	"	J. Duck	3.
Effie Moses	"	W. H. Oliver	3.
Fay Williams	Broughton	Joseph W. Carey	2.
Jennie Davis	"	Mrs Haynes	5.
Henrietta Morgan	"	Mrs H. Morgan	4.
Carrie Morton	Trounce Alley	Dodd estate	2.
Rosa Howard	Johnson St	A. A. Aronson	2.
Pauline Bockleman	Yates St.	Geo. Stevens	1.
Lizzie Lad	View	R. Austin estate	1
			38
Chinese women	Fisguard	W. L. Tiffken	About 100 women
" "	"	M. Hart	
" "	"	R. Porter	
" "	"	On Hing	
" "	"	Kwong Lee	
" "	"	J. P. Davis	

C. H. Bloomfield
Chief of Police

Police Chief Bloomfield's handwritten list of houses of ill-fame was likely not as complete as it might have been. *Victoria City Archives* although he estimated there were about 100 women occupants. And so his list was short—and it was one that in no way addressed those with a hidden financial interest in mortgages and other investments. Some prominent people were listed in his document, but most were already known to the city authorities—in fact, they were the very people who made and influenced laws, such as Provincial Minister of Finance Simeon Duck, city alderman Louis Vigelius, and former mayor and police officer Joseph Carey.

Some were owner-operators like Henrietta Morgan and Edith Haynes, while others on the list may not have fully discerned the nature of their investments. One example of this is Margaret Doane, the daughter of sea captain Joseph Doane and his wife Charlotte. Margaret's father died in 1883, as did her brother and only sibling in 1889, followed by her mother in 1890. She was left with their estates, including considerable real estate holdings. Margaret was known to write letters of complaint about the existence of houses of ill-fame, despite the fact she was renting to some. It is possible other people managed her affairs and she may not have realized this connection.

Brothels were a good investment if they were operated discreetly, and if they commanded high rents. Mortgages held interest rates as high as 18 percent, and there was no recourse to protest this. Bloomfield's list in no way gave any indication of just how involved many upstanding citizens were.

As for Henrietta, her health declined rapidly, and she died on July 30, 1886. According to the *Colonist* she was buried quickly with no service, and her death was deemed to be from natural causes. She was forty-seven years old.[3]

DEATH.—A woman known as Mrs. Morgan, the keeper of a house of ill-fame, died yesterday morning at 10 o'clock and was buried at 4 o'clock the same afternoon, the body being consigned to the grave without any funeral service whatsoever. The spirit which Tom Hood recognized when he wrote:

> "Rattle his bones over the stones;
> "He's only a pauper whom nobody owns,"

would seem to have been again illustrated in this summary treatment of the remains of this unfortunate woman. It was a significant and sad closing to a shameful life.

British Colonist, July 31, 1886

Henrietta's death and the subsequent wrangling over her estate and belongings reveal her connections. Her executor, Dr. Robert Barr Clark, claimed she had less than $300 in assets, but this was challenged. He admitted she had a $1,500 diamond ring but that it went missing after she died. Her creditors included the doctor himself ($1,000), Joseph Weiler furniture store owner ($179.10), John

Patmore Walls, her lawyer ($75), Wilson Brothers, for goods and services ($507.11), William Johns, expressman ($12.50), Henry Saunders and George Vienna, for groceries and liquor (amount not noted), and Pauline Massoulle, the lady's companion ($410).[4]

Henrietta Morgan's grave in Ross Bay Cemetery. *Photo by Linda J. Eversole*

Even Thomas Storey, the undertaker, had a claim for $113 for providing a shroud, coffin, grave case, cemetery fees, hearse, three carriage trips, express hire for taking the coffin to house and grave case to cemetery, three men to assist as pallbearers, and the undertaker's attendance.

Edith Haynes, new on the scene from New Westminster, came forward to say she was in negotiations with Dr. Clark to take over the property. The price was $5,000 with a mortgage of $3,500 and $280 in interest arrears. Edith claimed she had paid $500. As she already had possession, she then applied to the city for permission to put up a gate at the property entrance and was denied.

In the end, through the County Court and Supreme Court rulings, it seems payments were made. Edith got the property. A stroll through Ross Bay Cemetery shows a small, ornately carved gravestone to mark Henrietta's final resting place, stating her age as thirty-eight. Perhaps she wasn't a pauper, perhaps somebody cared, or maybe somebody found the diamond ring.

As Henrietta's time in Victoria drew to a close and her experiences in the world of the demimonde ended, another young woman was about to enter a path more dangerous and painful.

— *Grace's Story* —

(AKA *Trachsler, Harcourt, Jones, Brown*)

I FIRST CAME TO GRACE'S STORY THROUGH A NEWSPAPER REFERENCE to an attempted suicide by one of the inmates in a brothel. It mentioned she had been a bride in the city's first public wedding. I was intrigued and began to track her story through genealogy records, newspapers, and the records of the Ancient Order of Foresters (AOF), Victoria Branch.

Grace Trachsler was only eighteen in 1889, and her life at this point did not seem to hold much promise. Her father's death and her mother's "unexpected" pregnancy, leading to a crying baby boy in cramped living quarters for the three of them, did not bode well. They had only just arrived in Victoria from San Francisco, and her mother, Agnes, made a meagre living as a dressmaker. She had found employment doing piecework at her residence through her landlord's sister, who also did the same work.[5] It did not bring a steady income to the boarding house room they called home on Simcoe Street in James Bay, a two-storey frame house surrounded by empty lots.

The 1891 directory and 1889 map of Victoria show the house set a little apart from the cluster of houses in the outer wharf area of James Bay and surrounded by a large cleared field. It tended to be an area of workers associated with the docks, and their fellow boarders—mostly rough manual workers who needed their sleep—brought tension to an already uncomfortable living situation. In fact, the Trachslers had a celebrity sharing the premises: Former Middleweight Champion wrestler Jack [Tom] Connors was undergoing intensive training, utilizing the surrounding fields, for a much-heralded match against W.H. Quinn, the Pacific Coast champion. Many of Connors's fans gathered to watch his gruelling daily routine of outside exercise, skipping rope and lifting weights. But his efforts were to no avail as he lost the match. Quinn, his opponent, walked away with $500. It brought lively conversation to the boarding house, but it was not quite as startling as the news young Grace would bring to them—but then she was unpredictable.

Grace, an attractive girl, had found ways to get by and have fun too. Good girls were boring. The joyful escapades of drinking and carousing with the young men of the town were highly preferable to a stuffy room with a tired mother and fussy infant. She was particularly excited about attending the Ancient Order of Foresters' celebration at the park with her current escort, Percy. By sunset on Saturday, August 3, she would have an unexpected future to contemplate.

One of the most talked-about features of the Foresters' celebration was to be a public outdoor wedding. The weather was co-operating, and a couple was chosen to take part in the honour. The logical place was the Caledonian Society grounds adjacent to Beacon Hill Park and bounded on the southwest by Niagara and Government Streets. That was the plan as laid out by the Ancient Order of Foresters, who had devised the contest as part of their annual fête to entice young couples to apply for the honour. It was also a fundraiser to relieve the group of a pledge they had made to give the Royal Jubilee Hospital $200, which was well overdue and had become an embarrassment. In case that pledge might be forgotten, the Honourable Secretary of the Provincial Jubilee Hospital made sure a letter was prominently placed in the *Colonist* next to the AOF's advertisement for their upcoming celebration.

The events, which drew on the membership of the AOF throughout the province, began with a march through town with participants who had arrived on the train from Nanaimo and others who had made their way from the mainland. It was loud and colourful with a brass band, members in full club regalia, silk banners enlivening the crowd that lined the route along Fort Street to Douglas, then Humboldt and across the James Bay Bridge to the Caledonia Society grounds. There the Victoria contingent formed two lines and welcomed their brothers and the excited crowd into the festivities.

THE FORESTERS VS. THE JUBILEE HOSPITAL.

TO THE EDITOR:—I notice a correspondent of the Times this evening revives the question of the promised donation of $200 from the Order of Foresters towards the building of the hospital.

I may state I have been assured by some of the principal officers who have charge of their picnic demonstration at the Caledonian Grounds to-morrow that the matter has not been lost sight of, and that they fully intend raising the required sum during the day.

Due acknowledgement will of course be made should this desired end be attained.

WILLIAM M. CHUDLEY,
Hony. Secy. Provincial Royal Jubilee Hospital.

Victoria, B.C., Aug. 2nd, 1889.

Colonist, August 3, 1889

The decorating committee had done a good job building a raised platform with a canopy topped with the Union Jack and decorated by flower arrangements made from entries from the bouquet competition. The wedding was scheduled to take place at 4 PM, so there was plenty of time for the crowd to join in the various races—three-legged, sack, running, high jump, long jump, and sprints. As with their usual annual events there was an archery contest, the above-mentioned floral arranging, and a variety of foods and treats to purchase from local vendors. The crowd was large and boisterous and was swelled to almost double (an estimated 6,000 people) by the time the wedding was to commence.

Behind the scenes the AOF organizing committee was in a full panic, with the local newspapers reporting what they could glean from the jittery group. The betrothed couple had not arrived from Vancouver, and for some unnamed reason were deemed unsuitable anyway. An announcement was made that there would be a delay and that the wedding would take place at 6 PM.

With a huge sense of relief—and some desperation—the organizers had found one of their own members, Brother Sussex, who had recently joined, to volunteer that he and his young lady, Miss Grace Trachsler, would take the honour of being the bride and groom. What they didn't know was "Brother Sussex" was not quite who they believed, and Grace was not the virtuous bride they hoped for.

At 6 PM, Bishop Cridge from the Reformed Episcopal Church, perhaps harbouring some misgivings about the whole exercise, performed the solemn ceremony, and the couple walked back down the path festooned with flowers thrown by young children. Heartfelt cheers and applause followed them to their carriage where they set off having saved the day by providing the required spectacle.[6]

Five days later the AOF held a meeting, and a member revealed that Brother Sussex had given another name for the marriage ceremony. A committee was formed to investigate what was going on, and it was not until late the following month that the committee tracked him down and got an explanation. They discovered he was off the Royal Navy's Pacific Flagship *Swiftsure* but had left as being "unfit for situation." His real name was Percy Danby Harcourt—and yes, he had intentionally given a false name in his membership application. He was struck off the club rolls in October 1889 and eventually returned to his family home in England, abandoning Grace in the process.[7]

Grace's activities were bringing her into a life of disgrace. Her mother moved to Mayne Island with baby Robert, and she worked there as a housekeeper for the Collinson family, so any family support was gone. In the meantime, Grace had the attention of the police and was fined along with a known prostitute, Hattie Spalding, for "a buoyancy of spirits." The following year she was resident in one of the Broad Street brothels where, in a fit of despondency and addiction to morphine, she attempted suicide. On Thursday, May 29, 1890 she took a deliberate overdose. Her housemates were quick in summoning help, and Dr. Richard Morrison, whose office was located nearby, was able to bring her around and save her life. Almost to the day, one month later, she made a second attempt at ending her life, but once again quick action saved her.

Despite her young age her future was in great jeopardy, but thankfully she somehow managed to change things.[8] In February of 1893 she married a local businessman, William Henry Jones, a hotel keeper. He was thirty; Grace was twenty-two. They settled down, and William made a good living in real estate and later became the Dominion auctioneer. In 1895 Grace gave birth to a little girl they named Ida May. Ida May went on to attend the convent school in Ladysmith, as shown in the 1911 census; she later married and had a family of her own.[9]

What became of Grace and William is as yet unknown, complicated by the commonality of their names. There were several instances of the name William Jones in public records; the last information of Grace is on her daughter's death registration, where she is recorded as Grace Brown.

The Caledonia sporting grounds where Grace was married.
Victoria City Archives M07158

Grace was just one of many young women who found themselves desperately in over their heads with little support. Several young women over this period—those part of the demimonde—became addicted or alcoholic, and suicide attempts were all too commonly noted in the newspapers. In the 1880s there were more churches offering help to young women, and for some that was a way out of a life they could no longer easily survive. Even the police and courts would refer women to rescue homes as an alternative to prosecution.

— *Edna's Story* —

(AKA *Edna Farnsworth, Edna Bruton*)

THE ORIGINS OF EDNA FARNSWORTH (AS SHE WAS KNOWN IN Victoria) are mostly unknown, save for San Francisco newspaper references that were harsh and possibly not entirely factual. They do provide a starting point for her story. Edna died from a self-inflicted gunshot wound in Della Wentworth's brothel on Broughton Street in 1889. As was to be expected, the story made the local newspapers, but then was followed by newspaper accounts from San Francisco, a cosmopolitan city that would normally find this commonplace news, and whose Tenderloin was rife with tragic stories. The most likely explanation for the appearance of her story in newspapers outside of Victoria is that Edna was in some way connected to someone newsworthy.

The *San Francisco Examiner*, *San Francisco Chronicle*, and *Daily Alta* all reported on Edna's death, each giving a story about her time in San Francisco and putting more light on Edna's early life and the relationship with Della Wentworth. Reports claimed her real surname was Bruton; she had come to stay at a saloon/brothel at 108 Geary Street in San Francisco's Tenderloin, where she connected with Della. It was also here that young Edna, who was about sixteen at the time, met a local man, George Jerome Farnsworth, the son of a Michigan dentist with a large family. George lived with his brother Andrew and worked in his grocery store. According to the *Chronicle* Edna had run away from her boarding school, drank a lot with George, and then inveigled him into a marriage.

> *At a later hour, and while he was under the influence of liquor, she persuaded him to marry her, and the two repaired to the home of a notary public, whom they induced to draw up a marriage contract binding them together for life. It was the previous good standing and character of the young groom which gave the incidence importance.*[10]

This set me off searching genealogical sources in San Francisco, including census records, directories, vital statistics, school records, and anything else that might reveal clues about Edna's family. In the end I found nothing definitive except for a possible connection to a well-known salesman, Daniel Bruton, who travelled extensively and began a family late in life in the 1890s. Before he had this family with a wife thirty years his junior he lived near the Tenderloin in San Francisco. Daniel Bruton also had a brother George, who worked at the *San Francisco Examiner* newspaper. Another possibility was the Timothy Bruton family, but their children all lived at home. Any of these men could have been Edna's father. Birth or other records of an "Edna Bruton" of an age consistent with her Victoria information were not found, so her first name may be different.

No record has been found of a marriage between Edna and George Farnsworth, but George's second wife years later did acknowledge George had been married before, in 1887. Married or not, Farnsworth was the name Edna clung to for the rest of her short life.

What has been substantiated is that Edna and George lived in San Francisco at 418 Sutter Street, near Union Square on the edge of the Tenderloin district. George had been living with his older brother Andrew who moved out, and Edna moved in.[11]

Andrew bought a winery in the Napa Valley, where he accumulated businesses and property with great success. Edna and George soon parted company; again it was asserted by newspaper accounts that he moved north to get away from her, and she followed him. After this, all that is known for certain is that Edna appeared in Victoria, reconnected with Della, and then met a tragic end.

Edna made her way to Victoria in late 1887 and took up residence in a brothel on Douglas Street. From there she moved to Della Wentworth's place at 14 Broughton Street across from the Victoria Transfer Company premises. As would later be revealed by her doctor, James Helmcken, Edna claimed poor health, and Della made sure she was soon receiving treatment for unspecified complaints.

Della could relate to Edna's story as she had been the youngest inmate in the brothel of Marie Gordon at 806 Adams Street in Springfield, Illinois, when she was nineteen. Della reported she was born in Illinois, but no other family connections were found.[12] Della, like so many others, may have been recruited to work in San Francisco and from there made her way north and eventually to Victoria. She accumulated enough money to finance her own operation and rented the single-storey frame house at 14 Broughton Street from local contractor J.P. Burgess, and set about engaging the services of young women like Edna. Each woman had their own small room with a bed, dresser, hearthrug, and a window on the side with heavy blinds for privacy.

Inquest records provide a wealth of information, and in poor Edna's case they provide testimony that defines and elucidates her life based on the events of one evening. The handwritten notes of testimony in the words of the participants give detail to an otherwise closed world, with few records left to show the inner operations of a brothel, the inmates, and the clientele. It was a quiet night in the early hours of Sunday, June 23, 1889. Around 4:00 AM everything changed, and the inquest tells us how.[13] Edna seemed content to her fellow brothel inmates after spending time with one of her regular customers who made her feel, for a short while, loved and cared for—a rare feeling in those days, and one that only deepened a pain she carried inside. She likely knew she would never have a future with John Croft. He was a medical student working with Dr. Frank Hall and came from a prominent land-owning family in England.[14] She, on the other hand, would be considered a ruined woman, hardened by life experiences in a way that was difficult to hide. It was difficult not to give in to total despair. A tapping at her window momentarily distracted her and she pulled the blinds aside, but it was only Tom Hatton, the hackman, looking for John (or Jack, as he always called him). She told him Jack was gone, and then she abruptly closed the window.

A few moments earlier she had been in the parlour with John having lunch. Della Wentworth, along with Dot Gilbert and Effie Stone, joined them as no other clients were around. They testified that Edna begged John to stay longer but he declined, claiming another late-night appointment that to her could only mean a liaison with another woman. John had not even gotten into the Victoria Transfer Company hack—in fact, he was still conversing with the driver, Tom, who had found him near the side of the house—when they both heard the crack of a single shot. They ran to the front entrance where they found "Miss Dot" who exclaimed, "My God, Edna has shot herself!" They ran to Edna's room, where Della promptly passed out at the sight of the body on the floor. Tom jumped in his hack and went for Dr. Milne.

At the inquest the following day, Dr. Milne testified that at 4:30 AM he was called to the house, where he found a young woman of about eighteen or nineteen in a small room, lying on her back on the floor, her feet pointing toward the windows, with a great quantity of blood on the hearthrug beneath her. On closer examination he determined she was still breathing but had a bullet wound at the right temple in line with the eyebrow. With John and Tom, they lifted her onto her bed, where she died about five minutes later. Dr. Milne took the pistol that lay near her feet and set it aside for the police, who had just been called. The testimony continued with Dr. James D. Helmcken, who had also attended the scene as Edna's regular doctor.

> *I have attended the girl on one or more occasions lately and considered her of a very excitable disposition, and one who might commit suicide on any small provocation.*[15]

John testified he had a conversation with her, but things were fine between them and he didn't feel she was suicidal.

I cannot say what her idea was in shooting herself. I do not think that girl shot herself on account of my going out of the house; there was no trouble between her and myself.[16]

He then expressed hope that she would not have taken this action because of him—possibly revealing he knew her feelings for him ran deeper than he would admit.

Della revealed this was not Edna's first attempt at suicide and that she heard Edna often express that "she wished she was dead." Della had taken pistols away from her before but did not know she had one hidden away. The jury concluded the obvious: Edna "came to her death by her own hand, by shooting herself with a pistol."[17]

John Croft left Victoria a few months after Edna's death to continue his medical studies in Detroit. He briefly returned to Victoria to accolades on his sterling academic results, and as an avid amateur sportsman was chosen to present a championship trophy to local wrestler W.H. Quinn. He returned to Michigan, married in 1891, was sued for divorce in 1899 for non-support of his family, and died in 1902 at the age of thirty-four.[18]

George Farnsworth remained in California and married Jessie Lengille in 1895 in Los Angeles, where he worked in real estate. His deteriorating health led Jessie to commit him to the Stockton State Mental Hospital, where he eventually succumbed to paralytic dementia, a common result of advanced syphilis. His wife reported that two of his brothers had committed suicide. She also added to his death certificate that he had been previously married in 1887.[19]

Della Wentworth continued with business until 1892 when she left town and returned to San Francisco. It may well have been she who purchased the plot in the Wesleyan Methodist section of Ross Bay Cemetery, where Edna lies far from friends and family with a quaint tombstone and fence monument. Her funeral was well attended by those who felt compassion for the loss of such a young life and by the women who understood just how wrong things could go when you lived a life among the demimonde.

> *The funeral of Edna, the victim of Sunday's tragedy, took place from the house on Broughton Street where a service especially impressive and fitting was held by Rev. J.E. Starr. He referred briefly to the sad life and awful death of the young girl for whom he said no man nor woman could feel ought but pity; and his kind words which came straight from*

Edna Farnsworth's grave at Ross Bay Cemetery. *Photo by Linda J. Eversole.*

> *the heart went straight to the hearts of his hearers. The magnificent casket which enclosed the body of the poor unfortunate was covered with a wealth of flowers, while the treasures of the hot-house made fragrant the death room. The service at the grave in the stranger's plot in Ross Bay Cemetery was also conducted by Rev. Mr. Starr, the companions of the dead girl and a few sympathizing strangers following the body to its unmarked resting place.*[20]

It did not stay unmarked for long. An expensive tombstone was quickly raised with a fence surround. It stands today.

There is no happy side to this story as tragedy struck most of the participants, and the consequences of their life choices were harsh. As stated before, this was not an uncommon outcome—particularly for young women who could not imagine that a better life or any enduring love might come to them. We do not need to be in the room sitting on the bed with Edna to understand the feelings that brought her to raise the gun to her head and pull the trigger. What might be recognized today as depression or other mental illness too often was characterized as bad or immoral, particularly in the case of women.

This period in Victoria's development showed an increasing problem with drug addiction, as also shown in Grace Trachsler's life. Morphine was not uncommon, and opium was legally manufactured in Chinatown, where the smoking dens were not restricted to the Chinese residents.

Chapter Four

BROADS, BUILDERS, AND BANKERS

PROSPERITY AND GROWTH CONTINUED FOR THE CITY IN THE 1890s. Frame buildings gave way to handsome architect-designed brick buildings, and Broad Street was central to some of the activity. As the big buildings went up, the frame houses and shanties were displaced, and many of the small brothels were closed. This didn't mean it had become a respectable street, just a little more upmarket and mixed with more acceptable premises. Perhaps the most prominent building of the time was "Duck's Building," specifically built to house the carriage works of Simeon Duck, a long-time resident and community leader. Like Broughton Street, dominated by the Victoria Transfer Company buildings, this type of business employed many male workers, so having a brothel nearby did not seem to cause much consternation. Duck had been renting the space in his earlier buildings for many years to prostitutes—in fact, the whole block had many. Some transitioned their businesses to the nicer buildings when space became available. Some, like Vera Ashton, moved over from Broughton Street—it seemed a deadly place to hang out in those days—to take over the top two floors of this new structure. It was also good to have a landlord like Duck as his political and business connections meant anyone in his house was operating discreetly. It was likely one of the reasons Stella Carroll was drawn to the place. (See Chapter Five, Stella's Story.)

While conducting research on this building for my book, *Stella: Unrepentant Madam,* I was fortunate to be allowed by the owner, Michael Williams—a well-known Victoria businessman and supporter of heritage—to go over the plans and tour the building. And even more fortunate was the fact I had just come back from visiting one of Stella's relatives, her great-nephew, John, who loaned me a large photo that depicted two women standing on a staircase landing. On the back Stella had written, *The fatal hall and stairs of Victoria, BC. This is a hot time. Tusky and Howard, December, 1899.*[1]

This notation referred to the death of Marval Conn (AKA Emma Johnson) whose story features in the next chapter. By comparing the photo to the building layout of today, I was able to determine where the parlour was and the rooms used by the women. Although a wall has been put in one section and the stairway rails covered over, it is still possible to see the fairly extensive layout of the brothel.

Despite their quasi-legal status, the brothels that were emerging as semi-permanent establishments were complicated to run. There was a need for a full complement of women of a variety of types and natures. Some houses catered to men looking for women of different ethnicities. Also required was a housekeeper, cook (often drawn

The interior of the brothel in Duck's Building. This photo was taken by Stella Carroll in 1899. *Carroll Family Collection*

from the Chinese community), and musicians and entertainers to be brought in for special occasions and weekends; there were also medical and legal professionals to call in emergencies. Realtors and land brokers were needed for acquiring suitable property, while chattel mortgages were a way of obtaining credit for furniture and expensive clothing that couldn't be bought outright. When a madam purchased premises, they often secured money through private mortgages at exorbitant rates; this kept the transactions private but open for exploitation. Property owners leasing, selling, or providing mortgages used agents to conduct business, collect rents, and managc properties. In some cases taxes were paid by the renters rather than the owners to keep names discreetly hidden.

The madams, distrustful of the established order, eschewed bankers and kept their financial assets in jewels, particularly diamonds. Although normally reluctant to call the police for help, they did without hesitation when the jewels went missing. Madam Alice Seymour called the authorities in 1896 to report such a theft, as did many others in later years. They were rarely found; their desirable qualities as easily transportable liquid assets made them hard to locate when they disappeared. It was a huge financial blow when it happened—and it happened a lot.

As brothels became more established, so did churches, with two striking, dominant buildings erected in the 1890s. These buildings still stand. St. Andrew's Roman Catholic Church on Blanshard at View Street, and St. Andrew's Presbyterian Church at Douglas and Broughton, built in 1892 and 1894, respectively, were both surrounded by brothels. They were a great impetus for moral reform. In fact, the Moral Reform Association often had problems getting their members to follow through on prosecutions after identifying brothels and their clientele by surveillance. Nobody wanted to go to court to testify.

The churches' influence and agitation for change eventually brought a close to the brothels in their immediate vicinity.

St. Andrew's Roman Catholic Church was plagued with the presence along View Street of small brothels and shacks for itinerant workers. The church brought pressure to bear on the owners of these properties— in some cases members of their own congregation.

St. Andrew's Presbyterian Church was relentless in attacking the Broughton Street brothels. The church originally was on the corner of Gordon and Courtney Streets, kitty-corner to its new location. But the new structure was much larger and more imposing and a very tangible indication of changes to the downtown area. At least three of these brothels were adjacent to the neighbouring Victoria Transfer Company, which stopped renting the spaces and eventually bought out the one property they didn't own between the church and their stables. Effectively these

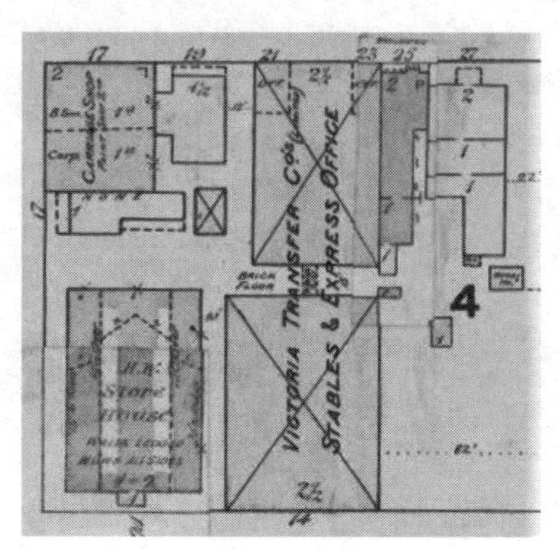

This portion of the 1891 Fire Insurance Plan shows the brothel of Dora Son (AKA Maud Lord) on the far right. The large empty lots next door would soon be the location of the new St. Andrew's Presbyterian Church. *University of Victoria*

two enclaves of sin were cleaned out, and the inhabitants moved on. One of the last to leave was Maud Lord, whose real name was Dora Son.

— *Dora's Story* —

(AKA *Eldora Palmer, Maud Lord*)

IN FEBRUARY OF 1890, THE STEAMER *ISLANDER* CARRIED PASSENGER Dora Son from Vancouver to Victoria. Whether she was alone is not known, but family lore has it that she was accompanied by a sea captain who promised a future he would not deliver on.[2] The previous ten years had been difficult, but Dora was hopeful better times were ahead now that she was on the other side of the continent and even in a new country. It seemed much farther away in time and distance from New York State and the town of Ogden in Munroe County, where she was born and lived with her father Dudley, mother Jane, younger sister Cora, and the Palmer grandparents. Ogden was a prosperous town at a peak of activity in 1855, when Dora was four years old. The Erie Canal, the transportation route bridging the Atlantic Ocean and New York City with the Great Lakes system, passed right through the town on the way to Lake Ontario.[3]

Dudley was a farmer and later a merchant, but in 1863 was drafted to fight in the civil war. He died in 1872, and Jane was left to get by as best she could. Eventually she moved in with Cora, who had married a local grocer, Addison Richmond.

Dora, now twenty, worked briefly as a servant for a local family but soon married a civil-war veteran fifteen years older than her, George Son. George had served with the 63rd Regiment of the New York Infantry; he was wounded in action and suffered health problems for the rest of his life. George and Dora took up residence in Albany, New York, where George established himself as a clothier. It was not a successful enterprise, so they placed their ten-year-old daughter Blanche in a boarding school in nearby Rochester and set out to explore the possibilities in the West.

In 1880 George and Dora passed through communities, staying in boarding houses in Kansas and then continuing to Colorado. By June 14 they were in Denver, Colorado, with George working as a commercial travelling salesman. Blanche had joined them but was likely a little dismayed at the ambience of the new locality, while her parents struggled to keep a home together.

George's health was seriously declining from chronic asthma, and Blanche, still a teenager, felt it was time to act. She took herself back to Rochester, married Charles F. Baker in 1888, and moved in with him and his parents, Solon and Mary. She then set about getting her father into the Milwaukee Home for Disabled Soldiers, where he was accepted in 1889.

Dora stayed in the West and now was moving toward a new start. She needed a home, and she needed to make money. With this fresh start came her new name, Maud Lord.

Whether or not the business of prostitution was new to her, drinking wasn't. Maud is recorded as living in a brothel, owned by Edith Haynes, on Broughton Street in 1890.[4] The timing wasn't good as Edith was dealing with John Anderson, the son of the proprietor of the Clarence Hotel; he was making a nuisance of himself mooning over one of the girls, Elvey Marston. Elvey, anxious to get away from the attention, travelled to Seattle with John close behind. She entered the brothel of Lou Graham, the most prominent and business-savvy woman in town, but John kept showing up determined to win Elvey's affections. She rebuffed him time and again, but it all came to a terrible conclusion at a saloon dance hall in Seattle. John followed Elvey there and pressured her to come home with him. She coldly turned her back to talk with another man. John reached his breaking point, ran up to a room over the saloon, pulled out a revolver, and shot himself in the right side, causing a mortal wound. He died twelve hours later. His father was devastated; it had been an ongoing fight for him to try to dissuade his son from fraternizing with girls like Elvey. The newspapers called her a beauty of the "blonde type" but with a decided lack of character. She was said to be seen hanging around the corridors of the hotel afterwards, "placing herself on exhibition and really seemed to consider herself quite a heroine."[5]

All this attention put a spotlight on 27 Broughton Street, despite the fact the events took place in Seattle. It was time to cool the operation, so Maud moved over for a time to Broad Street where she struck up a friendship with Grace Harcourt. (See Chapter Three, Grace's Story.) In early February 1892, Grace and Maud were caught and fined for speeding over the James Bay bridge; it may be imagined they were not being quiet about it. Maud appeared before the police magistrate, Farquhar Macrae, who noted that Grace was too drunk to appear.

After things settled over at 27 Broughton Street, Maud returned only to find more trouble was brewing. The same newspaper that chronicled her bad driving reported that a young man by the name of Porter had come to retrieve his seventeen-year-old sister from the brothel, claiming she had been seduced by a commercial traveller. He found resistance from his sister, who claimed she was "having too good a time."[6]

Both incidents, and the repeated mention of 27 Broughton Street, put the police in a position of needing to be seen to be doing something. So, they did. In September, two days of systematic raids focused first on View Street and then on Broughton and Douglas Streets. Police Chief Sheppard, two sergeants, and three constables divided up, and each took different premises. Sheppard handled Maud Lord's. In total they rounded up Lena Woodruff, Louisa Jones (AKA "the Countess"), and Maud as "keepers," as well as Claude Hunt, Lizzie Wilson, Stella Elliott, Stella Blanchard, and Lizzie Murdoch as "inmates."

Lawyer Samuel Perry Mills appeared for all of them, and the cases were tried at the same time. Mills was very clear and efficient in presenting his defense; he helped set the unofficial ground rules for the future on issues such as when warrants must be issued and what evidence was needed to prove a house was being used for immoral purposes. Not one to mince words, he added:

> *As to those who have complained about the places on View Street, let me tell those church men that some of the owners of the property in question are men who attend that same church. Let us stamp this thing out, but let it be done in a manly way.*[7]

It seems the court was listening, so Maud had every reason to feel confident if she operated discreetly the occasional fine was tolerable. It was the way with many of the other houses and was an unofficial business licence. In fact, it was a common practice in many other communities. She pled guilty and received a fifty-dollar fine and one hour of imprisonment. Added to this, the Moral Reform Association seemed in some disarray, so the pressure would surely lessen now.

There was no Quorum.

A meeting of the Moral Reform association was to have been held at the Y.M.C.A. parlors last evening, but only two members turned up, and as two do not constitute a quorum there was no meeting.

Daily Colonist, November 26, 1892[8]

Maud had found a home in Victoria and a friend in the proprietor Edith Haynes (AKA Belmont). In the summer of 1892, Jean Ray, a brothel keeper from Vancouver, moved over to take on management of 27 Broughton. Edith moved over to 14 Douglas Street to establish a new brothel that in time would come under the long-term ownership of Fay Watson. Jean perhaps thought better of the move, and in January of the following year transferred $3,000 of goods and effects to Maud Lord through a chattel mortgage.[9]

In 1896–97 things were calmer, and Broughton Street settled into a routine with little attention from the authorities. The Moral Reform Association had stopped their surveillance for now, and the churches had not yet been successful in removing the brothels. Although increasingly dependent on chlorodyne for chronic pain, Maud was managing well. She was confident enough to report a theft at her place, and based purely on a feeling she accused Fred Offerman, a businessman from Bellingham. The charges were dismissed as Offerman declared it was blackmail, and the court did not see the value in convicting based on Maud's guess.

It was an ill-advised move to bring herself to any court's attention, particularly as the town was once again becoming a busy place with rumours and movement toward a gold rush in the Yukon. Victoria was well placed as a transportation hub and for acquiring provisions. Change was coming, and an increasingly large influx of men on their own were roaming the streets looking for a good time.

No matter how discreetly Maud tried to operate, it should not have been surprising to her that the clergy and congregation right next door at St. Andrew's Presbyterian Church would use all the moral and political force they could bring to permanently close her down. The church was opened on January 12, 1890, with support from coal magnate Robert Dunsmuir and the provincial premier John Robson. They had weathered financial storms and were now on a stronger footing with a new pastor at the helm, the Reverend Leslie Clay. Church officials decided to step up the pressure on authorities, and the short respite of calm was ending.

Almost eight years to the day the church opened, Maud Lord was called to the courts and told she must close and vacate the premises immediately, not seeming to consider that she owned the building. She was charged with keeping a house of ill-fame, and she returned for a final court date a week later when she was fined twenty-seven dollars and told that next time there would be a jail sentence.

Dora Son at the Beacon Hill racetrack, ca. 1898. *Paynter Family Collection*

There was no mention of vacating this time, but she was informed that the premises must never be used for immoral purposes. The newspapers commented this had driven Maud into a deep depression, but the truth was more complicated. A few days later they reported on her death and now speculated that it was suicide. It was not; this was emphatically confirmed by the attending physicians Dr. George Duncan and his colleague Dr. James Douglas Helmcken.

Her official cause of death was meningitis as signed off by Dr. Helmcken.[10]

When a woman who was resident in a brothel died, suicide was the initial assumption. Some saw it as a kind of divine moral retribution at work. Possibly few knew the physical pain Dora—or Maud Lord, as she was known in Victoria—was barely tolerating. Chlorodyne, an opium-based mixture developed decades earlier as a treatment for any number of symptoms of a variety of ailments, was her only way of controlling the pain of meningitis; the doctors had indicated it was for palliative use.

Back in Rochester, New York, Dora's daughter Blanche was given the news of her mother's death, and she immediately made her way to Victoria. A handwritten will dated 1896 and witnessed by Edith Belmont (AKA Haynes) was found leaving everything to Blanche.

DR. J. COLLIS BROWNE'S CHLORODYNE

IS THE ORIGINAL AND ONLY GENUINE.

The Public are CAUTIONED against the unfounded statements frequently made, "that the composition of CHLORODYNE is known to Chemists and the Medical Profession." The fact is, CHLORODYNE was Discovered and Invented by Dr. J. COLLIS BROWNE (ex-Army Medica Staff), and so named by him, and it has baffled all attempts at analysis by the first Chemists of the day. The method and secret of the preparation have never been published. It is obvious, therefore, that anything sold under the name, save Dr. J. COLLIS BROWNE'S CHLORODYNE, is a spurious imitation.

CAUTION.—Vice-Chancellor Sir W. P. Wood stated that Dr. J. COLLIS BROWNE was undoubtedly the Inventor of CHLORODYNE.

CHLORODYNE is admitted by the Profession to be the most wonderful and valuable remedy ever discovered.
CHLORODYNE is the best remedy known for Coughs, Consumption, Bronchitis, Asthma.
CHLORODYNE effectually checks and arrests those too often fatal diseases—Diphtheria, Fever, Croup, Ague.
CHLORODYNE acts like a charm in Diarrhoea, and is the only specific in Cholera and Dysentery.
CHLORODYNE effectually cuts short all attacks of Epilepsy, Hysteria, Palpitation, and Spasms.
CHLORODYNE is the only palliative in Neuralgia, Rheumatism, Gout, Cancer, Toothache, Meningitis, &c.

From Lord Francis Conyngham, *Mount Charles, Donegal, December 11th*, 1868.

"Lord Francis Conyngham—who this time last year bought some of Dr. J. Collis Browne's Chlorodyne from Mr. Davenport, and has found it a most wonderful medicine—will be glad to have half a dozen bottles sent at once to the above address."

*** Earl Russell communicated to the College of Physicians that he had received a despatch from her Majesty's Consul at Manilla, to the effect that Cholera has been raging fearfully, and that the ONLY remedy of any service was CHLORODYNE.—See *Lancet*, December 1, 1864.

Sold in Bottles, at *1s. 1½d.*, *2s. 9d.*, and *4s. 6d.* each. None is genuine without the words "Dr. J. COLLIS BROWNE'S CHLORODYNE" on the Government Stamp. Overwhelming Medical Testimony accompanies each bottle.

Sole Manufacturer, J. T. DAVENPORT,

33, GREAT RUSSELL STREET, BLOOMSBURY, LONDON.

A newspaper advertisement for Dr. J. Collis Browne's Chlorodyne[11]

Blanche immediately opened the place back up as a boarding house while her husband Charles settled their affairs in Rochester and followed her with their five-year-old son, Carl. Two-year-old Lucille was placed in a convent house in Rochester temporarily. The family finally came together, settled in Seattle, but kept the boarding house going in Victoria. Over the intervening years Blanche rented the house on Broughton Street to the Japanese Methodist Mission Society and commuted back and forth to Seattle, where her husband continued to run a tobacconist and newspaper shop in the lobby of the post office building. When she finally sold the boarding house, she had accumulated enough capital to buy a noted resort on Orcas Island known as the East Sound Hotel for the sum of $12,000.

An unusual gravestone at Victoria's Ross Bay Cemetery, with Dora Son on one side and Blanche Baker on the other.
Photo by Linda J. Eversole

In 1954 Blanche died, and her family honoured her last wish to be buried with her mother in Victoria's Ross Bay Cemetery. The two had grown closer in the years before Dora's death. Blanche undoubtedly knew of her mother's activities in Victoria, and her choice to rent the house

Dora Son. *Paynter Family Collection*

Blanche (Son) Baker. *Paynter Family Collection*

to the Japanese Methodist Mission may reflect her feelings of disapproval and an attempt at appeasing the church. The house was used as accommodation for young Japanese men while the Mission helped them find permanent lodgings and employment, a purpose much more agreeable to the Presbyterian church next door. The very presence of the church was substantial enough to exert influence for change.

Victoria was a much different city now, with substantial buildings, well-established businesses, streetcars, and electric lights. The small single-operation brothels in frame shacks were disappearing, and some of the prostitution trade moved to hotels. Madams such as Alice Seymour, Fay Watson, and Jennie Morris, in their operator-owned houses, managed to keep on the side of the authorities and offered even greater discretion, keeping a tight control on alcohol consumption and steering clear of employing drug-addicted inmates.

Chapter Five

IMMIGRANTS, IMPOSTERS, AND INMATES

THINGS WERE HEATING UP IN MORE WAYS THAN ONE WHEN THE century crossed over into 1900. Authorities were discreetly trying to find a solution that would be palatable to all interests. These included religious, moral, health, legal, political, and possibly the most important and least openly discussed, financial business interests. All of these were very much a political agenda now, with the growing sophistication of the city, which required a balancing act between business and morality. At the very least, it was important to keep the sex trade more successfully hidden. Although it was no secret that the business of prostitution had financial input from prominent citizens, the incompleteness of the 1885 list of former police chief Bloomfield showed that there hadn't been serious attempts to suppress vice. Particularly as no action was ever taken against any of the owners.

Still, the police tried to contain the houses of prostitution, or at least those that were easily transitory. Owner-operator places with a high degree of discretion—such as those of Alice Seymour, Fay Watson, and Jennie Morris—were not targeted, but Jennie was induced to move from 14 Broughton Street to 19 Courtney to a house purchased by a Seattle colleague Virginia "Vinnie" Turner.

Virginia Turner was a young woman from the brothel culture of Seattle.[1] She was born in Ohio in 1876 and moved to Seattle with her mother Esther, and stepfather Charles, but by the age of twenty-four was working as a "seamstress" on a street of brothels. After accumulating some money, she bought a brothel on Courtney Street in Victoria in 1901 and partnered with Jennie Morris. By 1904 she had passed it all on to Jennie and made her way with her parents to Rossland and later Nelson, where she married William Turner and had two children. They ran a lakeside summer hotel on their ranch property. In later years, after her husband's death, she operated a hotel in Nelson and a restaurant in Vancouver. She married Fred Truslove in 1916, but she passed away two short years later in 1918. Like many madams, her ability to tell the truth about her age was comically varied, with birth years ranging from 1868 to 1881. She always kept them guessing.

By 1911, Broughton Street had been cleansed of unacceptable residents with the expansion of the Victoria Transfer Company and the construction of substantial buildings where the frame houses had been. Jennie Morris stayed on Courtney until 1912, Alice Seymour on Broughton until the same year, and Fay Watson similarly on Douglas Street.

In 1907, the police commissioners decided to set up a "restricted district" where prostitution could be carried on outside the city core. It was centred around Chatham Street and contained small frame shacks and cottages. Many took up residence in the newly created district and settled into business in modest but reasonably comfortable accommodations, feeling confident they would not be bothered by authorities. Some new places had been built, including a brick crib structure with a series of small rooms; this location had a resident caretaker, a Norwegian immigrant named Andrew Miller.

A steady influx of women came into the area—refugees fleeing the loss of their livelihood that followed the devastation of the San Francisco earthquake of April 18, 1906. Several of the newcomers had a few months' reprieve, getting settled only to relive the fires, devastation, and the loss of belongings and homes. On July 23, 1907, a fast-moving blaze started at the Albion Iron Works at about 2:30 PM around the corner on Store Street. Many of the women were just rising as their work was typically conducted through the night. The dry summer conditions and a strong wind set the flames racing through the neighbourhood.

Eyewitness accounts of terrorized, scantily clad women racing to save their belongings were reported in the press; one woman reportedly ran into the street sobbing, lamenting that she had recently been burned out in San Francisco. She believed this second visitation by fire was undoubtedly a visitation by Providence, and amid her heartbroken sobs, which left no doubt of her sincerity, declared her intention of hereafter leading an upright life.[2]

The more pragmatic dragged furniture, pianos, and other belongings out, but the fire was too fast-moving, and the destruction was quick and dramatic.[3]

The aftermath of the 1907 fire that destroyed Victoria's restricted district. *Victoria City Archives M07262*

Police Chief Langley announced that the restricted district was no more and that the women would just have to leave town. What did happen is that they dispersed to other areas of the city, including hotels and saloons, while those still outside the district—like madam Stella Carroll in Duck's Building on Broad—were not inclined to move anywhere for the time being. Despite Chief Langley's statement, the City directories show there was rebuilding of the restricted district houses, and they were still rented out to prostitutes, although the trade did seem to decline in subsequent years. It was no longer designated officially or unofficially as a restricted district, but as a blue-collar working area it still had a substantial clientele available.

— *Emma's Story* —

(AKA *Emma Johnson, Emma Trullinger, Marval Conn, Marval Ashton, Marie Ashton*)

IN VICTORIA SHE WAS MARVAL CONN, THOUGH WHY SHE CHOSE THE name will likely never be known. Stella Carroll would later say she had always known her as Mrs. Conn, and it was through research on Stella's brothel in Duck's Building that I first came across her story. At the time I didn't know that she was born Emma Louise Johnson on June 23, 1859, in Oconto, Wisconsin.

Her father, Charles Saxon Johnson, originally from Vermont, married Eveline Richards from Canada; they added to their large family as they moved on through Wisconsin, New Hampshire, and Michigan, necessitated by Charles's work as a carpenter and millwright. He also served in the American Civil War as a sergeant for the Union side in the 33rd Wisconsin Regiment. Emma was the seventh of their twelve children. By 1870 they'd headed even farther westward and settled in East Salem, Marion County, Oregon.[4]

The older children found occupations in the community, including jewellery and watchmaking. One undoubtedly unsettling event was the unexpected arrival of a half-brother born in 1874 to their father and his paramour, despite the fact he still lived with his wife. By this time Charles was still employed as a millwright and carpenter. Indiscretion notwithstanding he remained close to his children and continued to cohabit with his wife until her death in 1894. Surprisingly, the family now included this new arrival, Herbert, who is always attributed as a son of both parents. This seems unlikely as Eveline was fifty when he was born, and some records refer to him as a half-brother to his siblings. After the children were grown and their mother Eveline had passed, Charles Sr. moved in with his daughter, also named Eveline, and her husband, Charles High, a house carpenter. A dapper and energetic man, Charles Sr. continued as a travelling salesman of jewellery well into his senior years.

Emma's brothers and sisters found their places in the community, and young Emma had taken up with John Wesley Trullinger, a farm labourer from a pioneer family. They married on June 8, 1875 in the Commercial Hotel in Salem. The record notes one of the witnesses was Emma's father, who had given his permission as she was only sixteen. She gave her age as twenty-three; John was twenty-seven. A year later Emma gave birth to a son, Charles Herbert Trullinger.

In 1880 Emma moved back in with her parents and young son, the marriage with Trullinger having failed. As it was a census year she was recorded twice with different names (she went back to using her maiden name, Johnson). She gave three different years for her birthdates, her occupation was recorded as dressmaker as opposed to housekeeper, and her son was recorded as Herbert instead of Charley. She was enumerated with Truelinger [*sic*] in Jefferson, Marion County, and with her parents in East Salem, Marion County.[5]

In 1894 she was living in Portland again, calling herself Emma Trullinger, and declared herself a widow although John was still very much alive. Her son Charles, now twenty-two, was working as a clerk. In 1897 they moved to Northport, Washington, a railway and mining town seven miles south of the British Columbia border. Young Charles married Edna Curtis with Emma as one of their witnesses.

The fact that Emma is listed as being in this area may be indicative of her profession, as it was a mining town with very few women. This corner of northeast Washington was a prime area for mining and smelter work with the opening of the LeRoi Smelter and the proximity of the burgeoning mining towns of Trail and Rossland right across the US–Canada border. There is no specific evidence as to what she was doing, but as she doesn't appear in any records under the name of Trullinger it may be she was living under an alias. Three years later professional madam Stella Carroll would say she had known Emma for a while but understood her name was Marie Ashton and that she referred to herself as "Mrs. Conn." Stella was known to travel to Oregon—particularly Portland—on occasion and may have known Emma there. In any case, Emma kept her activities discreet and private.

A year after Emma's death, her son was still resident as a merchant in Northport and the town enumerator for the 1900 census. He was very clear to identify prostitutes as "sporting women" rather than use the usual euphemism of dressmaker. Openness was the best choice, as previously noted; Northport's female population was sparse, and a town of miners and smelter men would not likely require the services of a household of dressmakers.[6] A town like Northport did not need to worry about the political ramifications of brothels. They were part of the landscape, and clearly enumerator Charlie Trullinger was well aware of the business.

As for her time in Victoria, it was brief but dramatic. She lived in a handsome, well-constructed building known as Duck's Building—a step up from working in a mining town. It was common knowledge that owner Simeon Duck was a supportive and reasonable landlord for the business she was acquiring in his premises.

As previously mentioned, I came across Emma's story when researching Duck's Building in connection to Stella. I was intrigued to learn Stella acquired this business because Emma died on the eve of the property transfer. Research into Emma's family connections on Ancestry.com and the inquest notes to be found in the BC Archives produced a wealth of information to put together her life story—one that was unfortunately cut off at an early age. In the course of this research I was lucky to make contact with a relative who confessed they didn't know what had happened to her; they were pleased to get the information. They in turn provided what photographs they had of Emma's family, but sadly they could not find one of her.

Emma arrived just a few months earlier in the fall in preparation to take over the business. She undoubtedly found Victoria to be a most pleasant community compared to the grim aspect of Northport. She stayed with Vera Ashton, a long-time resident and brothel landlady who was seeking to move on. Accordingly, they reached an agreement for Emma to buy up all the chattels of the brothel operation at Duck's Building, with an understanding she would continue renting the premises.[7]

It was Christmas Day 1899, and after the party and sumptuous evening meal, the inhabitants were each heading to their beds. But Emma—or Marval, as she is called in the inquest testimony—previously too excited to eat, was now a little hungry. No doubt her mind was buzzing with ideas for the new enterprise she was embarking on and she wanted some company. She tried Stella's room on the second floor about 2:00 AM but didn't get any answer. She abandoned the idea but was still awake just after 3:00 AM and decided to try again.

According to the inquest testimony of the other women staying there, "Marval" headed to the parlour, calling out for the others to join her. Dorothy Carol headed there and found a much "put-out" Marval who had been unable to find the leftover turkey. Dorothy headed back to her room and Marval went to rouse the cook, Lee Toy, who had just made it to his bed after cleaning up and extinguishing all the lights.

Without questioning Marval, he went back to work. A very short time later he heard someone calling out; another Chinese servant and a woman were gathered in the hallway at the bottom of the stairs leading from the second floor to the third, where Marval's room was. It was still dark without lights, but Lee Toy could make out a form on the floor and felt a crunching under his feet of bits of a smashed lamp—the one Marval had been carrying. Stella was talking to the dazed woman, who went in and out of consciousness, telling her the doctor who had just arrived would send her to the hospital. Marval insisted she was fine and was helped to her room. Later that evening she complained of a pain in her head, and Dr. Gibbs was summoned again only to find she had died while he was en route.

The police, on information from the women at the brothel, contacted Emma's son Charles in Northport, Washington, and her father, Charles S. Johnson, in Portland, Oregon. Both men set out immediately for Victoria and arrived in time for the inquest.

At the inquest the women all testified to her being in good spirits, helped along by a modest amount of alcohol, and said that she did not have any bad feelings with anyone in the house and no grudges against her or held by her. Dr. Gibbs noted there were no suspicious marks on the body and that her injuries were all to the brain, which held a firm blood clot, and to her tongue cut by her teeth, consistent with her fall of a distance of four to five feet. "Her death was absolutely caused by a fracture of the base of the skull."[8]

Charles S. Johnson, father of Emma (AKA Marval), came to take her body home to Portland for burial.
Pam Tipton Collection

Despite the fact the women were well acquainted with Emma, if a little uncertain about her legal name, her father and son opted for the painful task of identifying her body. The affidavits accompanying the inquest show that they knew she used the names Marval Conn and

Marie Ashton but that her real name was Emma Louisa Johnson. They also stated that Charles Herbert Trullinger was her only son and heir and that she had divorced John W. Trullinger in April 1899.

The paperwork was soon sorted, and her bereaved father took her home to rest with the family, alongside her mother and eldest sister, Eveline. Charles S. Johnson joined them in 1915 when he passed at the advanced age of ninety-six years and ten months.[9]

Emma's son Charles and his wife moved back to Oregon, and he continued to work toward becoming an optician. Eventually he carried on to Honolulu, Hawaii, where he started a very successful optical business. He died at the young age of forty-two in 1918.

As for the brothel, Stella Carroll stepped in and took over the chattel mortgage, and to Vera Ashton's relief took over the operation of the brothel immediately. It was to be her first business in the city, but certainly not her last.

— *Stella's Story* —

(AKA *Estella Hannah Carroll, Curtis, Durlin, Bearns, Fabian*)

IT WOULD NOT BE POSSIBLE TO WRITE A HISTORY OF VICTORIA'S brothel culture without mentioning Stella Carroll, possibly the most fascinating and pre-eminent madam in the city's history. In 2005 my book *Stella: Unrepentant Madam* was published; there was a second printing in 2013. The records of her journey from her birth to death, which I followed with dogged determination, yielded information over a twenty-year period that revealed a woman who likely would have been successful at anything she put her hand to. For the purposes of this book I will give an overview, but the details of her very eventful life are contained in *Stella*, which also includes an extensive bibliography and footnotes providing the source material. For the context of this look at the development of the business of prostitution in Victoria, she must mentioned with her interwoven connections to many of the people profiled.[10]

When I started researching Stella, I did not have the advantage of digitized documents and access. I wrote countless letters to various agencies around North America, sent faxes, and made phone calls. I had no photographs of her, only descriptions from people who knew her—an archivist and pioneer resident (Ainslie Helmcken), a bartender and messenger boy (Cecil Temple), and a nurse who knew Stella in her final days. I did have the advantage of being a government research officer, with greater than public access to information in land titles and government records still not easily obtained. Then I traced her family, with some difficulty, working with the common name of Carroll. With luck and serendipity it all came together, and I travelled to California to meet Stella's great-nephew and the family historian, John Carroll. I was amazed at his and other relatives' generosity in lending me photographs and even her autograph book. I walked through rooms that contained her silver punch bowl with devil's head ladle and cups, wondered at the coat rack that appears in one of the photos of her Victoria brothel, and admired the large oak table with the lion's head feet.

Stella, as she was called by family, friends, colleagues, and even the authorities, was born in the small town of Bourbon, Missouri, in 1873, the eldest of four children. She was largely the caregiver for her siblings Roy, Minnie, and Harry, and their bond was lifelong. Their mother died when Stella was fourteen, and their father's restless nature saw them heading out from the comfort of family and familiar surroundings to travel westward to Kansas and Oklahoma, where they participated in the Oklahoma Land Rush and acquired property for their father's livery stable.

This is when Stella's entrepreneurial spirit was first stirred. She set off alone in acquisitions, dabbling in land ownership and development at a very young age, encouraged and helped along by men who admired her spirit and shapely figure. She wisely invested in land along the Atlantic and Pacific Railway that terminated in Los Angeles and passed through New Mexico and Arizona in communities that were quick to see opportunities. Albuquerque, Gallup, Flagstaff, and Winslow came to know young Mrs. Curtis (she had married a Gallup general contractor). She did very well and was shrewd enough to keep much of it in her name. Dudley Curtis turned out to be a raging jealous abuser who on more than one occasion hit her in the presence of others. She had no problem getting a divorce.

She married again, but it was short-lived, and in 1894 she went to San Francisco to explore ways of building on the money she had acquired. Already she found herself with more funds than she had ever thought possible.

Stella was a serious businesswoman, as this photo taken in San Francisco shows. *Carroll Family Collection*

She sent her two brothers to a private boarding school and sister Minnie to get a teaching certificate, thinking to set them up for life. It turned out they were as rebellious and strong-willed as Stella; they ended up taking different paths from what she had envisioned, but they always remained connected to their dear sister Stella.

Every bit the businesswoman, Stella allied with famed San Francisco madam Tessie Wall and saw the potential of establishing a high-class bordello, just not in competition with the two principal madams of the Barbary Coast, Tessie and Jessie Hayman. In 1899 Stella went north, spurred by the development occasioned by the

Yukon gold rush, and she found herself by invitation in Victoria at a Christmas dinner with some of her new and old acquaintances.

It was the shocking and untimely death of Emma Johnson (AKA Marval Conn) that galvanized Stella to seize on her vision of making the best brothel in town in Duck's Building. The eponymous Duck was all for it.

Stella was very quickly a part of the scene and knew well many capitalists who could help her along—Simeon Duck being the first where others would follow, happy to provide financing. Between 1900 and 1908 she expanded her holdings to several buildings and properties in the downtown area, the red-light district when it got going, and a handsome country home/parlour house on the Gorge. She endured all the political and judicial vagaries and many times thought to leave. Her sister Minnie had built up a brothel clientele in Albuquerque, jointly financed with Stella, and in one of her low times Stella sent a postcard showing her disillusionment with the possibilities of Victoria.

> *Dear Siss: back to the cactus with me—if matters don't change. Things did look good once & may again. E.C.*[11]

In the end she stayed on, with trips to Europe, visiting family in America, and special events like the Rose Festival in Portland for respite. She endured abusive customers, difficult employees, violent lovers, and a new husband (for a time). She fought with politicians, entertained visiting sports teams, and catered to local businessmen. She lost her temper in court, drove her carriage too fast, and most devastatingly of all lost her leg in what was a shadowy incident of either abuse or accident. Minnie did have some concerns from afar about her sister's temper and suspected alcohol might be playing a part. Rather than broach it directly, she sent her a comic postcard which proclaimed, "If Drinking Interferes with Business Give Up Business," but added, "Get wise kid and get off the coyote wagon [southwest slang for the police wagon]."[12]

In time Stella went back to San Francisco to take over the impressive Union Square brothel of the retiring Tessie Wall. She arrived just in time to be raided and charged with treason under a federal law that had harsh penalties for brothel owners within a certain distance of a military camp. In the case of San Francisco, it was the Presidio.

As age crept up on her she ran a boarding house and married one of her boarders, twelve years her junior. She reunited with family and enjoyed visits with her young nephews and nieces. This happiness was fleeting as her husband was killed in an accident, and she found herself living in Northern California in a small cabin with cats, rabbits, and the occasional neighbour for company. She died there in 1946 and is buried in Los Angeles with other family members, where her gravestone reads *Beloved Sister*.

It was the end of an era. Neighbourhoods would no longer tolerate brothels, no matter how impressive the houses they occupied. Some women still felt hopeful that they could stay quietly, but it was not to be. A newly instituted policy of deportation threats were quite effective in moving along the trade from American women. It did take some time, and some were more than willing to take on the fight for the lucrative rewards they imagined could come their way. Even the City of Vancouver looked into setting up a restricted district in 1912 that attracted American women who could see a good investment. In Victoria, American women establishing brothel businesses became less of a problem as some of the long-established American madams began to move away or retire.

Chapter Six

DETECTIVES, DEPORTATION, AND DEMIMONDES

THE MORAL REFORM MOVEMENT WAS GROWING NATIONALLY with concerns about the number of American citizens facilitating the business of prostitution. In 1907 Dominion Police Force Detective Edward Foster was sent to make a three-month inventory of practitioners in Vancouver and Victoria. In Vancouver he identified eighty American women as either prostitutes or madams, and they were promptly ordered out of the country. His work in Victoria showed it was a similar situation. Some panic ensued, and women were instructed to leave town immediately or face formal deportation when they appeared in court.[1]

This continued on well into the onset of the First World War, and some women took to lying about their citizenship, claiming nativity to Canada. Their lengthy police records and the newly established mugshot system counteracted the deception. Better communication between police departments and the exchange of identifying features became a normal part of dealing with the "American problem." Mugshots were routinely distributed to major police forces.

Martha Roberts and Lizzie Cook worked for Stella Carroll and later went to Vancouver. *Vancouver Police Museum and Archives*

By 1910 Victoria had a substantial population in excess of 30,000 souls, and municipal politics was a great facilitator of pushing for reform. Political interests came down to two competing camps—basically the business elite who focused on discrediting the current mayor, and the moral reform proponents who elected Alfred J. Morley in 1905–1907, 1909–1911, and again in 1913. The years between reflect the triumph of the business-backed candidates. In an effort to unseat Morley, moral reform groups were provoked by rumours and outright accusations of payoffs and kickbacks to the mayor, police commissioners, and police, designed to undermine their support of this moral reform candidate. A letter printed in the *Times* newspaper and attributed to "John Smith" accused the mayor of not suppressing vice and called for an investigation of the police and licence commissioners.[3]

In March the moral reform movement had garnered enough support and power to pressure the provincial government to investigate allegations made against the Victoria Police Commissioners—allegations that included the mayor. A commission established under the direction of Judge Peter Lampman commenced in the spring with over thirty witnesses summoned to testify to prostitution and gambling activities in the city. It was a colourful array of people who paraded through the courts. Madams, prostitutes, gamblers, police officers, reformers all took their turn at describing the situation from their individual perspectives.

Pudgy Raymond was brought from San Francisco by Roma Graham (Lillian Gray) and was arrested with her in Vancouver in 1912. *Vancouver Police Museum and Archives*

As far as prostitution was concerned, the testimony determined a pattern of property ownership sometimes hidden behind "agents" to disguise the real owners, exorbitant rents, and protection money paid to authorities. One unidentified woman of the demimonde testified that she knew the "uptown" houses of prostitution were paying for protection despite others who denied protection money was paid at all. Otherwise, she said, they would not have been permitted to remain outside of the restricted area. She further declared she had been told by her attorney that she could secure protection through an Italian who, she said, owned premises on Chatham Street. She had tried to find this man, but had failed. Asked how he secured his protection, she stated that she supposed that he "salved the palms of the officials" and the money went to the police.[4]

Other witnesses, in particular Dr. Ernest Hall, sounded an alarm based on health concerns rather than moral or religious concerns, or concerns of corruption among officials. His testimony concluded with a startling statement:

> *One bad woman in a community [is] worse than having bubonic plague, rabies, smallpox, scarlet fever and diptheria together, he said.*
>
> *That's pretty bad, observed Judge Lampman.*[5]

The solution of deportation was having some impact, and women who had been well entrenched in their business here looked for opportunities to return to their own countries. San Francisco was well into rebuilding after the earthquake and had opportunities for those with the means to invest there. Seattle had opportunities now too, with the death of the grande dame and politically well-connected Lou Graham who had ruled the demimonde for many years. For some it was time to retire, but others were determined to take up the challenge and continue to stay in British Columbia, if not Victoria.

One of these tenacious individuals was a bright, beautiful, and formidable woman who went by many names but in truth was Lillian Gray of Illinois. Lillian's connections to Victoria are documented by a notation on her mugshot and arrest records that she was in Victoria using the name Nellie Foster. She knew Stella and worked with her but set her sights on Vancouver with word that an official restricted district was in the works. I chose to include her because her story is a very colourful tale of a woman who, like many others, came to British Columbia with money and determination to succeed. She appears in the end to have rejected Victoria for her business, but her story is a good example of a woman who, like Stella (and perhaps even a little feistier), would not quit until she decided.

Mugshot of Lillian Gray, AKA Roma Graham.
Victoria Police Museum and Archives

— *Lillian's Story* —

(AKA *Lillian Gray, Roma Graham(e), Louise Grainger, Nellie Foster, Lillian MacDonald*)

LILLIAN ALWAYS TOOK A GOOD PICTURE. SHE WAS AN UNDENIABLY attractive woman, and even in her lowest moment, a mugshot taken at the Vancouver Police Station, she still pulled it off with style. She managed to get a hint of movement in the final frame, likely to make sure the record was blurred. Her hat was plain, yet tilted to one side to give her a rakish look, and her large eyes peered out with a dark and defiant glare. She'd spent a few years in the trade, and by this time she knew the ropes. She would have known that even set back as she was, she would soon be back in business, making money like she always had.

Lillian Gray, ca. 1899. *Gray Family Collection*

Lillian was a long way from Tampico, Illinois, where she had run a store with her mother, Alice, and sisters, Maude and Allie May. The local newspaper had hailed them as being among the many women entrepreneurs the town boasted.

> *We will risk the assertion that there are few towns in Illinois that can boast of as many lady proprietors and clerks engaged in stores as there are in Tampico at the present time. To prove this we will enumerate them, starting with Mrs. J.T. Gray, and her daughters, Allie, Lillian, and Maude.*[6]

It was a nice compliment, but a truth born of necessity. Lillian's father, John T. Gray, was a retired farmer and a Civil War veteran of the Union Army Company B in the 58th Illinois Infantry. As indicated in his Civil War records, his health was permanently damaged through this lengthy service wherein he saw action in ten battles. When he returned home, he married a local girl, Alice Slye, and in time they were blessed with their three

A Gray family portrait. Lillian is second from the left, her hand on her mother's shoulder. *Gray Family Collection*

daughters. In early 1887 John's health declined significantly, and he died on March 27 of that year. In his obituary he was lauded as an "honored and respected citizen, a true husband and a kind and indulgent father."[7]

The girls and their mother managed to carry on in the small village of Tampico, located 180 kilometres west of Chicago, with their grocery store located on the main street. In 1894 Alice acquired property in Sandwich, Illinois, a suburb of Chicago, where she and the girls set up home in a small house. Maude, the youngest, eventually met a local man, Keeler George Leet, and marriage was soon in the offing. Allie May, who was also a qualified teacher, worked with her mother. It was Lillian, the middle daughter, who was restless and prone to dark moods and discontent. A poignant note from her sister Maude showed the compassion she felt for her sister.

> *I sincerely hope that in times of sadness, to which you are somewhat prone, you will draw consolation from the many beautiful things herein written and that in your pensive moments this journal will sooth* [*sic*] *away your heartaches and lift your soul from its melancholy musings.*
>
> *—Your sister, Maude*[8]

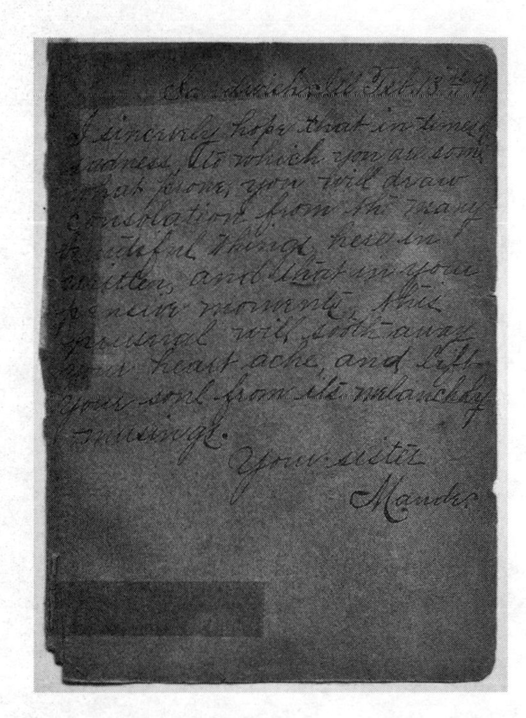
Sandwich Ill Feb 13 [illegible]

I sincerely hope that in times of sadness, (to which you are somewhat prone, you will draw consolation from the many beautiful things herein written, and that in your pensive moments, this perusal will sooth away your heart ache, and lift your soul from its melancholy musings.

Your sister
Maude

A book inscription believed to have been written by Maude, addressed to Lillian. *Gray Family Collection*

The 1900 US Federal census records a woman named L.R. Graham living in one of the famous brothels of San Francisco at 223-25 Ellis Street, run by the notorious Jessie Hayman and another madam, Olga Evans. She had a birthdate of May 1875 and claimed to have been born in California. In later years L.R. Graham became Roma Graham and was revealed to be Lillian Gray, who many times used this alias.[9]

How this leap from small-town storekeeper came about is lost in the details, but Chicago was a leading purveyor of vice second only to San Francisco. At the same time as Lillian appears in San Francisco, sisters Ada and Minna Sims, calling themselves the Everleighs, opened one of the most famous upscale brothels in American history. Whether Lillian had any connection to them is unknown, but she likely would have been familiar with their names. The "Everleighs" themselves had close connections to San Francisco. At the very least they were possibly an inspiration.[10]

Lillian ran the 223 part of the Ellis Street brothel with three other women ranging in age from nineteen to twenty-one, with origins in New York, England, and France. Jessie Hayman, herself from Florida, had six girls aged nineteen to twenty-seven, from Nebraska, Oregon, England, and Mexico. Olga Evans had retired.

Things seemed to go well for several years, despite the occasional violent encounter—including a stabbing that made the newspapers in March of 1906. William F. Hopkins was charged with stabbing James McGinley, a local boxer, who had punched him when he hit Roma Graham. Corroborating witnesses confirmed Hopkins had hit Roma, and even she had to admit it was true—although she did so reluctantly, calling him a good friend of four years. The trial had many witnesses, and accusations were levelled at Hopkins's mother, who was said to have tried to bribe McGinley to drop charges. In the end Hopkins went to jail, though not for long.[11]

On April 18, 1906 it all came crashing down, literally, when the earthquakc hit. Thc premises at the corner of Mason and Ellis Streets were devastated. The catastrophe that ensued in the city

San Francisco earthquake damage at Mason and Ellis Streets, the corner where Lillian's brothel was located, 1906.
Library of Congress

was so severe that prisoners, including Hopkins, were released from jail to help families struggling to cope.

Although others fled out of town, Lillian stayed. This was to be a new beginning and many others agreed. As soon as things were back in control and cleanup underway, small hotels began popping up. One of them, at 166 Turk Street—two blocks from the old establishment—was under the management of the newly invented Roma Graham. She had a steady clientele, six years of experience, and connections to authorities and some of the city's elite.

While she waited for her hotel to be built, she rented premises at 1324 Golden Gate Avenue. She still was under scrutiny and put up with a couple of convictions and a $100 fine for operating a brothel. In one instance she spoke too quickly, pleading guilty before the judge noted in a puzzled voice that there was no evidence of this. As she pled guilty, he was forced to fine her. It seemed like an unfortunate mistake, but it may have been a strategy to protect one of her supporters. One of the people caught in the raid was Victor Magnin, son of the well-known Magnin family of high-end clothing store fame. He was questioned as to whether he had financial interest in the brothel and in protecting the madam and her inmates. He denied this and another accusation that he had tried to influence the police. The case ended abruptly when Roma pled guilty, saving the Magnins from further embarrassment.[12]

In 1907 Roma took possession of the newly built hotel at 166 Turk Street that she christened "The Graham." She was open for business, supplying rooms to travelling entertainers and running a brothel. It was a popular place, attracting a wide clientele, but brought problems right from the start. In 1908 one of her "boarders," Agnes Lambert, was poisoned with carbolic acid by someone who had taken her out for a carriage ride. The next month Roma reported a theft of her jewels, two diamonds valued at $4,000. Police Chief William J. Biggy took personal charge of the case after she arrived at his office and was reported to have been in conference with him for an hour. He sent his men out to lock the exits of what the paper described as the "notorious resort," and all the inmates in the house were searched (fifteen women and a dozen men). No trace of the gems was found. Notifications were sent to police stations along the coast but to no avail.[13] It was a huge financial loss, but Roma had some consolation in the form of a rather impressive lover.

Young, handsome, famous, and a money-maker, boxer Stanley Ketchel (AKA the "Michigan Assassin") was the talk of the town. He arrived for a much-anticipated run of matches and made the Hotel Merritt on Geary Street his home base for at least a year. Roma was fifteen years his senior, but her beauty belied her age. His career soared with his successes, and he was considered one of the greatest middleweight champions of his time. He was great friends with Jack Johnson, the famed Black heavyweight champion who managed to cross colour lines and find success. They were both known for their love of drinking, frequenting brothels, and beautiful women. They were opponents too, and in preparation for an upcoming match, Ketchel, whose career had been slipping, boarded at a ranch to concentrate on training. In 1910 he was murdered by a ranch hand in a set-up situation where he was accused of rape, but in fact had been

Stanley Ketchel, boxer, middleweight champion, and Lillian's lover. *Wikimedia, Library of Congress*

robbed and framed. Police notations and newspaper reports linked Roma as a paramour of Ketchel.[14]

In 1910 it was census time again, and this time Lillian used the name Roma Graham on her entry. She declared she was born in Texas in 1875, was divorced, and ran a rooming house for the theatre industry. She had seven other women living with her, aged twenty-two to twenty-seven. It was a time of political turmoil among authorities in San Francisco, and the previous few years had seen a growing crackdown on vice. It was clear 166 Turk Street was no boarding house or hotel. Nor were these girls' ages necessarily correct. Then newspapers reported on one runaway, Lois Spencer, who was found at Roma's place. She was fifteen.

It was time to explore other opportunities, maybe even another country, and Roma set off for Vancouver and Victoria, British Columbia, around 1911. She may well have heard through the well-connected and informative grapevine of brothel keepers that Stella Carroll, from the old San Francisco days, was doing quite well. Roma set off with her current lover James Mulligan (AKA Reynolds), who had been living with her, to explore new opportunities. Mulligan was a notorious con artist or bunko man specializing in bogus land deals and investments, and he was known as a dapper dresser. On his arrest upon returning to San Francisco, after one of his journeys in 1909, he was called the "King of Bunko Men." The reporter, with much admiration, noted the Parisian suit and diamond tie pin he was wearing as he was hauled off to jail.[15]

Roma heard of a good opportunity in Vancouver, where the authorities were setting up a red-light district, and decided to look at the possibilities. She found a place to run, but was swiftly convicted in 1912, forfeiting the $250 bail she had paid. Much to her annoyance, her photo was taken and a card was made to go with it, detailing her previous known crimes. She gave her name as Roma Graham, birthplace as Toronto, and stated her age as twenty-nine—suggesting a birthdate of 1883, a far cry from the truth: 1871.

Lillian Gray's house on Alexander Street in Vancouver. *Photo by Linda J. Eversole*

Undaunted, she immediately purchased property on Alexander Street and put money into having an architect design the house. She took out a building permit for #504, although the next year an additional permit was issued for #512 for apartments and rooms—the owner's name recorded as L. Gray, and architect Wilson & Wilson, at a cost of $17,300. It was to be two storeys with twenty-one rooms, three private bathtubs, thirteen taps, thirteen basins, and six water closets.[16]

As Alexander Street was frequently a cacophony of sound with all these substantial buildings going up, Roma headed over to visit Stella Carroll in Victoria. They met up at Stella's downtown brothel at 643 Herald Street and spent the night drinking and conversing with another woman and the occasional male visitor. It was a quiet night, and Stella had even sent some clients over to the country brothel, Rockwood. She had business cards printed for such occasions, and they provided entry to her more exclusive property.

Even though nothing was going on, they were horrified when the police suddenly came crashing through the door. The three women and the Chinese cook, Quong, were paraded out to the jail—straight past members of the Purity League, who had been keeping the house under surveillance. Stella bailed Quong and herself out but left Bessie Moore and "Nellie Foster" (as Lillian was calling herself) to stew in jail overnight. They were just furious enough to testify against Stella, who was subsequently convicted while they each paid a fifty-dollar fine. This moral reform pressure was enough to convince Roma to head back to Vancouver to the designated red-light district.

A few months in, the authorities decided that a red-light district was not a good idea, and despite Lillian's declaration of being born in Toronto, there was a move to get her deported. Not wasting any time, she approached one of her regular visitors, a young Englishman named Geoffrey Woodhouse, who called himself a real-estate broker; she married him on March 4, 1913.[17]

By September federal authorities were diligently pursuing this case, and it was followed in the local press daily with updates highlighted and first-page features. Lengthy articles, many on page one, followed the legal technicalities of the case throughout the court proceedings in September 1913, with headlines proclaiming

> *Must Cross Border by Four O'clock, Says Judge*
> *Law Unable To Find Notorious Courtezan*
> *More Legal Tangles in Roma Graham Case*
> *Roma Graham Scores Another Legal Victory*
> *Holds Roma Graham Free to Stay Here*[18]

Roma was famous—they even knew her real name, Lillian Gray, now Woodhouse. Despite this, she was always called Roma Graham. Column after column detailed her lawyer's manoeuvrings and the authorities' frustrations.

On September 18 it came down to the immigration officials having a mere four hours to find Roma, put her on a train, and get her across the border before her lawyers could file papers to appeal the deportation orders. Immigration Inspector Malcolm Reid, accompanied by Superintendent of Immigration William Hopkinson, left the courtroom before the proceedings closed and rushed to her residence, only to find she had slipped away minutes before and eluded them. Meanwhile her lawyer, Elmer Jones, was in a fast car heading to the New Westminster courthouse to file a new application for habeas corpus to protect her from being arrested.

Newspaper columnists, with a hint of admiration, described her as having been in Vancouver two years and in constant conflict with the law—a slight exaggeration. They spoke of her infamy up and down the Pacific Coast and wrote about the property on Alexander Street that was now bringing in a rental of $1,200 a month. It went on to describe her as the "consort" of the late Stanley Ketchel, a prizefighter killed in a row over a woman, and went on to refer to Roma's many convictions for offenses against public morals. The best part for Lillian may have been when they described her "as only a girl in years." She was forty-two.

Her marriage to the mysterious Geoffrey Woodhouse, a British citizen, was also examined, with quotes from Mr. Justice Morrison on how it was a pure artifice such as is prevalent in Shanghai,

> *where certain persons, anxious to escape the jurisdiction of the courts, will advertise a bonus for men to come and sacrifice themselves at the altar of matrimony.*[19]

No one had been able to locate him for the past two months. Did he exist? In fact, he did. There is a marriage registration that confirms he was born in Shropshire, England; he was then living in Vancouver and later headed to Australia.

On September 23 it all came to an end. Lillian, resident at the Empress Hotel in Victoria, nervously awaited the outcome while her lawyers, D.G. MacDonell and Elmer Jones, made their plea to Chief Justice Hunter of the Supreme Court. Hunter, who was known to be lenient with the demimonde, reviewed Justice Morrison's views on "the marriage," and while he agreed that it may well have been a ruse, expressed his view that it really didn't matter. The marriage was lawful, she had become a Canadian citizen by reason of that marriage, and it was enough to prevent her deportation. He added a rebuke:

> *It is a reproach to our civilization that when the immigration officials found that this applicant had become a Canadian citizen these proceedings were not dropped. The zeal of the immigration department has outrun its discretion.*[20]

Before the year was out, Geoffrey and Lillian were divorced, and she was back on Alexander Street. The following year she moved up to a small frame house at 1043 Georgia Street that was raided, and once again she was convicted of being a keeper of a house of ill-fame. It was time to leave, and she headed back to San Francisco.

This is when records on her become less easy to find. She did marry perhaps more than once. As I learned from one of her family members, they understood she had been married to a man named Fox. It was a joke in the family that Lillian was playfully known to them as Slye (her mother's maiden name) Gray (her maiden name) Fox (a married name). When she returned to reside permanently in Illinois, on the death of her sister Allie in 1936, her name was Lillian MacDonald. Their mother Alice was still living and transferred the portion of the property that she shared with Allie to Lillian, who moved in with her. Alice died in 1940, and Lillian moved in with Maude and Keeler and later Maude's daughter, Blanche. In correspondence with the author, Blanche's daughter Judy tells a story that has been handed down about the independent and outspoken Lillian:

> *Lillian and my mom were in the same hospital at the same time—she was sick, and my mom delivered my older brother. My dad went to see Aunt Lily in the hospital and told her of the new baby boy. The story goes that a single tear came down her face. She died a day or so later. I heard that story many times.*[21]

In 1948, the infamous and formidable Lillian Gray (AKA Roma Graham) passed away and was buried beside her mother Alice and sister Allie at the Oak Ridge Cemetery in Sandwich, Illinois. She was

The grave of Lillian MacDonald, formerly Gray, Oak Ridge Cemetery, Sandwich, Illinois. *findagrave.com*

seventy-seven, as noted on the registration of death, which finally listed her true birthdate of April 4, 1871.[22]

This look at the connections of Vancouver's Alexander Street and Victoria just before the First World War was serendipitous as it brought me to a story of a couple whose lives likely crossed with Lillian's. Violet Vickers, later to be revealed as Alice Young, was a prostitute in a house just down from Lillian's and was at the centre of a particularly violent event—the nature of which was not unknown in a restricted district. I took note of it and then was fortunate to find mugshots of her and her husband in the Vancouver Police Archives. Her story and the photos were part of a presentation I gave to the Vancouver Heritage Foundation several years ago. I came across her again in Victoria research some years later, again in a record of violent circumstances, and I felt compelled to find out what had led her to such a life.

As I had information that she originally came from England, I started searching through genealogy sources to find her. I was successful in tracing her family origins and her immigration to the US.

— *Alice's Story* —

(AKA *Alice Hughes, Alice Young, Violet Vickers*)

FOR ALICE HUGHES, AGE SEVENTEEN, THE JOURNEY ACROSS THE ocean must have been an adventure of unlimited horizons, perhaps clouded with apprehension.

It was 1909, and the SS *Corinthian* sliced through the water, making good time for its scheduled arrival in Quebec. Alice travelled with her mother, also named Alice, sister Janet, and younger brother John. Their father—who worked as a wooden pattern maker in the town of Thornaby, Yorkshire—was not with them; he may well have been deceased. Records state that the destination for Alice and her children was Salt Lake City, Utah. It would not be a long stay: By the following year the whole family was in Tacoma, Washington, where Alice's sister Janet married Herman Kruschke, the owner of the Bee Hive restaurant. It provided employment for the whole family.[23]

Life seemed promising for Alice. Police records describe her as having blue eyes, brown hair, and a slender five-foot-four-inch frame. She had caught the eye of a young Scotsman named Archie Young. He seemed a good match, seven years her senior with a steady job as a car man for the Tacoma Railway and Power Company. They became very close and married on January 5, 1911, a necessity brought about by Alice's increasingly obvious condition. Their son was born three months later.

The SS *Corinthian* brought Alice and her family to the United States in 1909. *Courtesy of the author*

Sadly, death records show that on April 20, little Archie—named for his father—died. Newspaper reports from Vancouver revealed the background of what led to their subsequent domestic difficulties. After losing her baby, Alice ran away. Archie searched for her and eventually got a tip that she was working in Vancouver, British Columbia, in that city's notorious red-light district. He found her at 614 Alexander Street in a brothel run by madam Mary Scott.

He gained entry under the guise of concern and civility, but it was soon apparent he was determined to take Alice, now going by the name Violet Vickers, home. He reasoned, cajoled, pleaded, and finally threatened until the morning hours, but to no avail.[24]

Overwhelmingly frustrated, he left, but returned that afternoon for a final showdown. He carried a revolver. Refused entry by one of the inmates, Billy McCartney, Archie shot his way into the house. Panic ensued as Archie made his way to the second floor and commenced shooting into the street at the police, who had arrived quickly, and the fleeing brothel girls and their customers, including a passing messenger boy. As the police began to rush up the stairs, he pushed them aside to make his escape, just narrowly missing them, but wounding Alf the messenger boy, who had come a little too close to observe the scene. Archie, now shot in the arm, made a break for it and ran toward Powell Street, stopping behind a telephone pole to reload. A second police bullet stopped him, but he

Alice's mugshot taken in Vancouver, BC.
Vancouver Police Museum and Archives

Archie's mugshot, Vancouver, BC.
Vancouver Police Museum and Archives

was not fatally wounded. In best western shoot-out fashion, he reportedly called out, "Boys, you've got me."

When taken into custody, Archie was immediately taken to hospital, where his shattered ankle meant amputation of his right leg below the knee. A suicide note was found in his possession; in it he declared his intention to "snuff" out the girl and himself. Mugshots were taken of Archie and Alice, and Archie was charged with wounding with intent. Surprisingly, he was eventually released, the thought being that he had suffered enough with his traumatic amputation.

Despite this violent occurrence, Alice found compassion for Archie and they attempted a fresh start. Their story continues with information from Victoria newspapers and inquest testimony to come.

Not wanting to return to Tacoma, they decided to try Vancouver Island and found a place to rent in Victoria. Archie struggled to come to terms with his physical disability and was only able to get work as a teamster and in some labouring jobs. His dependence on crutches meant intermittent work, and he became increasingly despondent. Alice found employment working in Stevenson's candy shop on Douglas Street, but it did little to ease their financial situation.

They moved a couple of times and struggled to keep a roof over their heads. Archie in his darker moments had suspicions that Alice has returned to her old ways, and it festered in his mind when she was absent, particularly when she went off on a short trip to Seattle.

He planned to go there himself to get an artificial leg fitted, but before that happened, she had returned home, and they moved ever closer to their fateful end.

Tuesday, May 12, 1914 was a sunny day—good weather for Parfitt Brothers Construction to continue their work on the Bay Street Armoury. Sidney Petch was a cement finisher, and according to his later account to the coroner's jury he was engaged in the rough work when he was startled to hear a noise behind him.

> *I was working near the Field Apartments yesterday morning between 11 and 11:15. I was on the sidewalk. I heard a cry like a baby. I did not pay any attention but when I heard it again I turned around and saw a woman coming out of the apartments with blood over her breast. She threw up her arms and fell on the sidewalk.*[25]

Petch leapt into action, alerting his fellow workers, and ran to provide help. Hot on his heels was his boss Mr. Parfitt, who with lightning speed had managed to find bandages and a blanket to wrap around the stricken woman. Police Constable Thomas Hastings arrived about the same time as Dr. Greaves appeared, and they bundled her into the patrol wagon and rushed her to the hospital.

By this time the deputy chief of police, Thomas Palmer, had arrived on the scene. Palmer and Dr. Greaves, followed by Petch, Parfitt, and a growing posse of police and workers entered apartment #2 with some trepidation. They found Archie clad only in undershorts and undershirt, sprawled half on the bed in a pool of blood flowing from several wounds.

> *I found a razor in the bed, it was under his left side, was open and near his left hand. Most of the blood was on that side of the room and that side of the bed . . . both sides at the foot of the bed were clear. There was . . . money in his clothes.*[26]

Although he was unresponsive, there were faint signs of life and Dr. Greaves quickly summoned transport to the hospital. By the evening's close, as was expected, both Alice and Archie had succumbed to their wounds. At the coroner's inquest the next day there was much discussion to determine who was perpetrator and who was victim, in part based on the position of the razor found by Palmer. In the end all they could conclude, based on the evidence presented, was that it was a murder-suicide.

Constable Littlefield volunteered that he had known the two of them for well over a year, so it was his testimony that provided identification. He also made a point of adding that Archie was not addicted to drink. In a sad twist of fate, a telegram from Alice's mother was found on the floor saying she would be arriving the following day. A police officer met her with the tragic news. Fortunately, Alice's sister Janet had come too, and they spent hours going over the events with detectives and expressing their disbelief that Alice could be capable of such violence. Despite the fact the inquest jury had not determined the sequence of events, the *Daily Colonist* newspaper put forward a theory held by many.

> *Constant brooding upon the woman's mode of life is believed to have been the motive which led Young to murder his wife and then kill himself. In September last Mrs. Young was leading a disorderly life in Vancouver.*[27]

As an old friend had testified at the inquest, Archie had been despondent for some time. He was working as a teamster in construction but had been off work for three months. This gave him plenty of time to dwell on a painful disability while observing other young men boldly going off to war or gainfully employed on the large construction site right outside his window. Perhaps it was the humiliation of a wife driven by economic need to supplement their income that was too much to bear.

A recent photo of the Field Apartments, the scene of a murder-suicide.
Photo by Linda J. Eversole

A burial plot for Alice at Ross Bay Cemetery was arranged, with the strict stipulation that Archie was not to be interred with her. Her funeral was attended by her mother, sister, and a couple of friends. His plot, paid for by the city, lies a short distance away.

The turn of the century and the years leading to the First World War saw the economic base of Victoria change. In *Geographies of Sexual Commerce* historian Patrick Dunae explains,

> *The sealing industry, which had employed hundreds of men who lived in residential hotels near the waterfront in Victoria, was shut down by an international treaty. The Royal Navy base at nearby Esquimalt closed in 1905, and with the closure, several thousand bluejackets, who used to spend their leave and their money in Victoria, were lost to the economy. At the same time Victoria's manufacturing industries were declining in face of vigorous economic growth in Vancouver.*[28]

Business in the downtown core was cleared of any obvious sexual trade. According to Mayor Alfred Morley in his annual report for 1913, the suppression of vice was successful. This of course was combined with the numbers of young men heading overseas to fight, so the male population that might have been patronizing the brothels and cribs severely declined.

> *The morals of the city [had attained a] high standard and everything possible had been done to prevent questionable characters from locating in the city.*[29]

George Perdue, detective on the Victoria police force, reiterated this in his report of 1915, in which he stated that of the eighty-three women that had been interviewed and advised to leave the city, most complied.

While moral reform had taken a back seat in the issues of day and was supplanted by the outbreak of war, it remained a factor that would grow when soldiers began returning.

Chapter Seven

THE REFORMERS

Reformers come in all types, with a variety of motivations. Right from the earliest instances of vice the reformers were there to raise the alarm. In Victoria, from the 1840s to the 1860s, this was largely led by religious leaders of the Roman Catholic, Presbyterian, and Methodist churches. They focused their rhetoric on moral degradation and unsanitary conditions, which in the town's early stages of development was a way of attacking the growing Chinese population and the Indigenous people. As in any community unsanitary conditions came from a lack of resources, poverty, and being disadvantaged from the larger society. While this may have been the case in the earliest period it also included many of the industries that employed a large number of working men of all nationalities. Small cabins, shanties, and rudimentary shelters were used by working men as well, whose standards of cleanliness might well, have been at odds with a church leader. The emphasis on the Chinese and Indigenous populations was just as much about land possession and property values. As for moral degradation, by the standards of church leaders, that was found amongst many of the population.

The Methodist Church took the lead role, with the Reverend Ephraim Evans decrying the influence of the dance houses and the moral decay he postulated went with their presence. In the 1870s, with an established constabulary, law enforcement was a tool to maintain order but was not effectively used toward eliminating the problem. The 1880s and '90s saw the rise of rescue homes and the beginnings of organized moral reform organizations. The turn of the century, following on the grassroots work of rescue and suppression relating to vice, brought the issue further into the political arena, with business interests challenging reform candidates. It was not just a local issue: In 1884 entrepreneur and lawyer Joseph McNaught ran for a position on Seattle city council and explained to the newspapers his view on prostitution and business:

> [The] *cornerstone of the business prosperity of the cities of this coast rests on the saloons, the gambling houses, and the houses of prostitution; these are woven and interwoven with every branch of business. When you strike them, you strike at the business interests of the whole community.*[1]

While he may have had a point at that time, in the 1900s moral reform took on greater strength with organizations emerging and becoming more active. Religious, cultural, health, and even financial interests came into consideration, and there was no shortage of individuals and groups ready to bring forth and fight for their ideals.

There were many groups, but the following were formed as follows: The Temperance and Moral Reform Association (1890); Ministerial Association (1888); Central Union of Christian Endeavour (1893); Voter's League (1902); and the Purity League. These were all active through the 1890s and for decades onward. Many pushed their agendas through political means and supported moral reform candidates such as Alfred J. Morley, who served as mayor of Victoria from 1905 to 1907, 1909 to 1911, and in 1913.

> *The Capital City is agitated at present by a movement inaugurated by some of the most aggressive pastors for purging the Augean stables of the city's social evil. An association called the Temperance and Moral Reform Association has been formed.*[2]

The Women's Christian Temperance Union was formed in Victoria by the 1880s, with dedicated and energetic members ready to make changes. One of their first goals was to provide a refuge for women who wanted to escape a life of degradation and vice. They raised funds and purchased a home at 108 Cormorant Street for $3,000. They had rooms for twelve women, mostly there by referral, although they wanted to recruit women directly from houses of ill-fame. To this end they printed out cards to leave and went calling at the brothels to talk and pray. It was a good-hearted attempt, but their success was not great.

> *Any mother's girl wishing to escape from a sinful life may find friends, food, shelter and a helping hand to a better life by coming just as she is, at any time, to the* REFUGE HOME NO. 108 CORMORANT ST., VICTORIA, B.C.
>
> *The mission is* NOT IN ANY SENSE A PRISON. *Inmates wishing to leave may do so at any time. Gospel Service of song every Friday night commencing at 8 o'clock. Come and welcome.*
>
> *Committee of Management* [3]

As with the Chinese Rescue Home, one of the controversies that surrounded it was whether the inmates had the free will to leave if they wanted. It would be an ongoing issue for both the rescue homes.

The Legal Council of Women of Victoria in Vancouver Island articulated their concerns around "social evil" in a resolution passed in a December 1906 meeting to consider what steps could be taken to help "unhappy sisters," a term spoken with deep "Christian feeling". The idea of anything outside of their own beliefs of what constituted a happy life did not seem to be a consideration.

For the most part rescue homes operated with either some success or too much controversy. One notable exception was the Chinese Rescue Home at the time of John Endicott Vrooman Gardner[4] and an interested party by the name of Professor Walter Rufus Menzies.

— *Gardner, Menzies, and the Chinese Rescue Home* —

John Endicott Gardner. *First Metropolitan United Church Archives, TF_2004-0144*

IN 1885 THE PRESENCE OF BROTHELS and what were believed to be "slave girls" galvanized more concrete action in the form of the establishment of a Chinese Rescue Home. This initiative was led by John Endicott Gardner, a San Francisco immigration agent who had lived in China. He was fluent in the language and was one quarter Asian himself. He came to Victoria to work as an interpreter but stayed on to find a solution to what he felt was an alarming situation. In partnership with the Reverend John Edward Starr, a Wesleyan Methodist minister, and working with citizens from prominent families (all white), he set up a facility on Pandora Street to provide sanctuary to women and girls fleeing deplorable conditions and enforced servitude.

The difficulty was that on the surface this seemed a noble cause, but it was far more complex than imagined. Despite Gardner's familiarity with Chinese culture and language, his plan did not consider the needs or even aspirations of the women themselves; it was primarily a case of creating domesticated individuals for marriage or restricted types of work with Christian values. Much the same attitude had confronted the First Nations who acted as partners but found oppression, racism, and imposition of a societal norm that did not value or include their own culture and beliefs. As the rescue home was founded on the tenets of Christian beliefs and Victorian morality, these were the overriding guiding principles. The home had mixed success and, as one would expect, some fierce opposition. Gardner even complained that Police Chief Bloomfield was not providing any support for the home, hinting that he might have been paid off by Chinese business interests.

Gardner did have support from individuals both within the Chinese community and outside among the larger society. One of many who supported the work was an acclaimed magnetic healer who had recently arrived from the San Francisco area. Professor Walter Rufus Menzies took up residence, accompanied by a woman believed to be his wife, Jennie; according to their accounts they supported Gardner and his work—even taking some girls into their own home as domestic help. But the collegial acquaintance between Gardner and Menzies would soon sour.

What appears to have been unknown at the time—and even in recent accounts—is that only one of these men was truly a reformer, while the second was a criminal of the worst kind. In brief it came down to John Gardner publicly accusing Professor Menzies (in the *Victoria Daily Times*) of trafficking girls:

> *The Times of Wednesday and last evening contains lengthy statements concerned with the alleged trafficking of Chinese girls by Professor Menzies . . . The charge reduced down to facts is that the Professor sold a Chinese girl, formerly an inmate of the Chinese Home to a Chinaman for $150 . . .*
>
> *Professor Menzies is also accused, in company with a certain Mrs. Crawford, with having spirited away another Chinese girl, Ah Loy, to the other side of the line ostensibly with a view of selling her to the owner of some Chinese house of prostitution. The girl was seen in his company on the Rithet, dressed in European clothes and with her face daubed with pigment for the purpose of deceiving the public into the belief that she was an Indian girl.*[5]

Shelly D. Ikebuchi's well-researched book *From Slave Girls to Salvation: Gender, Race, and Victoria's Chinese Rescue Home, 1886–1928* provides a good summary of the cross-accusations and defenses of Gardner and Menzies, and their supporters and detractors through the rival newspapers of the *Victoria Daily Times* (pro-Gardner) and the *British Colonist* (pro-Menzies). This growing scandal spawned a series of editorials, letters to the editors, quotes from filed affidavits, and a lot of outrage and subsequent defense.

As accusations from Gardner and Starr flew at Menzies, he left the city. Although the passenger list printed in the *Colonist* only shows Jennie Hopkins and Zoe Menzies, their young daughter, en route to California, the papers later revealed Professor Menzies travelled on the steamer *Yosemite* to Vancouver and made his way overland. Gardner, enraged by this turn of events, tried to have Police Chief Bloomfield charged with allowing Menzies to escape.

As the rhetoric flew, one notable letter to the *Daily Colonist* newspaper—purportedly sent by Jennie after she returned to her Oakland, California, home—staunchly defended her husband's actions and character. It also outlined accusations of her own against Gardner. She started by expressing surprise at the charges, claiming that she and her husband never did anything that Gardner had not done himself by aiding young girls from the rescue home to find suitable marriages and then recouping the expenses from the groom. She went on to describe an incident of two of the girls running away from the rescue home because they had been beaten. She and her husband offered to take one of the girls into their own home and find a home for another. She implied and outright accused the rescue home of mistreatment and imprisonment of the girls while painting herself and Professor Menzies as rescuers.

> *On the 14th of January last the two girls in question ran away from the Home to Mrs. L.M. Fowler's house. They complained*

> *of having been terribly beaten and nothing would induce them to return to the Home. That was Saturday. Mrs. Fowler waited all afternoon and up to midnight, expecting someone to come and see if they were there. She had been their matron. No one came or made any inquiry whatever about them.*[6]

The information about this incident came from an affidavit filed by Mrs. Fowler's daughter Jessie, not Mrs. Fowler herself. In it Jessie states that Professor Menzies's mother-in-law followed Mrs. Fowler as matron but was replaced by Mrs. Annie Leake.

Whether Jennie had actually written the letter was called into question—and subsequent research has found that that was a valid query. Jennie B. Hopkins was in fact not married to Menzies, and she lived with her widowed mother in Oakland; Zoe Adelle, her daughter with Menzies, died in 1890 from an extreme inflammation of the throat. Whether Menzies had any further contact with Jennie is unknown, but they never did live together again. In time she moved on, married a successful lawyer, and likely never crossed paths with Professor Menzies again. She may never have known a letter attributed to her had caused quite a stir in Victoria in 1888.[7]

This letter, printed verbatim in the *Daily Colonist*, elicited much reaction from the citizenry, the authorities, and individuals with associations to the rescue home. Gardner did not participate in the rhetoric, but Reverend Starr, who himself had a sterling reputation that no one questioned, did weigh in about Gardner's character, calling him

> *. . . not infallible. Like other men he has his faults . . . Knowing as I do the Real Truth, I deem it an honor to say I could trust him with my life.*[8]

In the end Menzies was charged with kidnapping two young Chinese women, Loi Ho and Ah Lin, and found guilty of "procuring a girl under twenty-one years of age to have carnal dealings with a Chinaman." He was sentenced to eight months in jail, despite the plea that he had a wife, an aged mother, and a newborn daughter awaiting him in Oakland.

Despite this positive vindication, a disillusioned Gardner and his wife returned to San Francisco once their second child was born. He went back to work for the Immigration Department continuing his work in rescue and reform.

Interest in Menzies dropped off once he was incarcerated, but he featured in one last sarcastic newspaper story after his release.

> *The report that Professor Menzies had returned to Victoria turns out to be incorrect. He is nestling safe in the arms of Uncle Sam at Blaine* [*Washington State*] *and pathetically telegraphs to his landlord at Vancouver to forward the valise that he so hurriedly left. The professor is not likely to return to John Bull's*

> *dominions for a few days at least. The "magnetic attraction" is not in that direction. If we are not mistaken there are other semi-pious frauds in the province that will soon be called upon to change quarters—and that quite suddenly.*[9]

In contrast, the citizens of Blaine were overjoyed with his return:

> *Prof. MENZIES, the magnetic healer, very much pleased his friends in Blaine by returning here Monday and taking up several cases which he was before attending with marked success. He will in future make his permanent residence in this part of the world, attending patients in British Columbia and on Puget Sound.*[10]

Previous local news items were full of testimonies to his magnetic powers with even the local doctor singing his praises. Menzies continued his itinerant practice along the coastal communities as far as California and into Vancouver and New Westminster on the Canadian side. His home base was now Whatcom, where he once again rented rooms. Although he had cultivated a practice that kept him employed as a healer, an incident occurred in Whatcom that revealed his true nature. On July 30, 1896, the local newspaper reported a violent attack that took place the evening before when an irate group of local citizens pursued Professor Menzies down the street. He sustained a bullet wound in his foot and was taken into custody. Court records reveal what prompted this outrageous act in such a small quiet community. The following day, Menzies was charged with bastardy, amended to attempted rape of a nine-year-old girl, "Birdie," the daughter of a local fireman.

> *Prof. Menzies sojourned in the city jail last night and narrowly escaped severe punishment at the hands of irate citizens who had been apprised of his infamous doings, which doubtless led to the shooting affair of the night before. He will doubtless be criminally prosecuted. He has served a term in jail in British Columbia and has a most unsavory record in California.*[11]

The charge revealed he "did beat, bruise, wound, and ill-treat with intent to violently, forcibly and against her will unlawfully and feloniously to carnally know and carnally abuse." The attack took place on July 19th, but he was not arrested until the 29th. Her young siblings testified, but the details of the attacks on her and later on Menzies have not survived in court records.[12]

He served an eight-month sentence in Whatcom County Jail and was released on April 18, 1897. The 1900 census shows him still in the area in the village of Fairhaven, renting rooms from a local family. Menzies claimed to have been born in Canada in 1843, and his profession is listed as general agent. Within the year he was arrested for practising medicine without a licence. Released on bail he disappeared, possibly moving to Everett, Washington. He reappeared in the 1910 census, retired and living in Sacramento, claiming to have been born in New York in 1841. A Sacramento death record for W.R. Menzies in 1911 shows a birth date estimated as 1830.

Even with Menzies's later offenses unknown, it is interesting to read the *Times* characterization of his crimes:

> *. . . a terrible outrage upon society, an infamous wrong upon humanity, and a scandal and disgrace to the community in which, in the broad glare of day and under the very noses of the guardians and enforcers of the law, it has so brazenly been enacted.*[13]

There was limited success in the rescue homes, and while there was emphasis on religious and domestic training, and eventual employment in the community, other reformers focused their concerns on the health perspective. Foremost among them was Dr. Ernest Amos Hall.

— *Dr. Ernest Amos Hall (1861–1932)* —

DR. HALL WAS A HIGHLY RESPECTED MAN OF STRONG OPINIONS. HIS career had given him what some might consider a pragmatic approach to moral reform, with a focus on the issue of public health risks. The prominence of venereal disease was one such concern, but he also noted the high incidence of alcoholism. All of the brothels were purveyors of alcohol as much as sex, and in fact the consequences of serving alcohol without a licence could be more serious than running a house of ill-fame. Dr. Hall took this a little further in his treatise *The Truth About Alcohol* with the following statement:

> *A brain poisoned with alcohol becomes callous to duty and leads to a disregard of sense of honor and rectitude of dealing. Those who lead immoral lives frequently depend upon alcohol for this deadening of conscience.*[14]

Ernest Hall was born into a farming family in the Halton region of Ontario in 1861 and was the youngest of six. He attended medical school at the University of Toronto before continuing his postgraduate work in Edinburgh and at some German medical clinics. He married Maria Louisa Fox in 1885 and set up his practice in Northern Ontario, eventually moving to Victoria in 1891. Although raised as a Baptist, he converted to Methodism and worked with religious leaders of that faith to bring about changes in laws and suppression of what he considered vice.

In 1904 he moved his office, clinic, and residence to the former home of newspaper editor D.W. Higgins, Regent's Park, on Fort Street and eventually operated the Restholme Sanitarium there from 1910 to 1913. He was controversial and very active in advocating for gynecological surgery to alleviate mental disorders.

His perspective on moral reform was based on health concerns, and he was quoted in an article in the *Victoria Times* of October 7, 1910 with the headline "Drastic Order By The Police – Disorderly Houses Ordered to Close – Immoral Women Must Leave Their Haunts on October 31 Next." Dr. Hall, whom they described as a prime mover for closing the restricted district, expressed alarm that a large percentage of the male population was "being ruined physically as well as morally".[15]

In his role as a leader in the fight to close the restricted district he, by necessity, was politically active and was a diligent watchdog on the authorities. Shortly after the First World War had ended, he questioned the actions and motives of several members of the Victoria Police in their enforcement of laws, prompting some to sue him. Many of these accusations were unfounded, but by now it was common knowledge that there was corruption in the police force. Bribery was not unknown from the earliest of times, and Dr. Hall and his supporters focused on this aspect and that of health safeguards, as the actual establishments of prostitution were disappearing. Dr. Hall died in 1931 lauded as "Lover of his Fellow Man."

The impending war to be known as World War I or the Great War and its sacrifice of young men would be the most defining event in pushing the success of moral reform ahead throughout the continent. Major red-light districts in New Orleans, Chicago, New York, and San Francisco saw motivated political change take hold, and these areas soon disappeared. Vancouver quickly closed its red-light district on Alexander Street before it had even got going. Victoria's Chinatown kept on as before; after the fire the Chatham Street area was rebuilt but only continued as a place of sexual commerce for a few more years. Prostitution was largely driven into hotels and onto the streets. The age of the utilitarian brothel and even the grand carriage house was coming to an end in Victoria. Stella Carroll transferred her house Rockwood to her brother Roy, who lived in it with his family. When it was destroyed by fire in 1923 he subdivided the property and a number of houses were built on the former grand estate.

Moral reform in the time leading up to the war was much more an issue in the United States than in Canada. In fact, many communities including Vancouver and Victoria had successfully driven the trade into discreet and hidden operation. For that reason it still held an appeal to some American entrepreneurs. One of these entrepreneurs left a striking remnant of an ambitious endeavour that was literally in the wrong place at the wrong time.

A particularly notable house—designed by Thomas Hooper, one of the city's premiere architects of the early twentieth century—was purpose-built to serve as brothel when constructed in 1913. At the time it might have made sense, being located near Beacon Hill Park and the connection to the demimonde who used it as a stroll and the parade of carriages that passed by, sometimes at exorbitant speeds.

Anyone who likes to walk around the waterfront on Dallas Road and the margins of the park today cannot miss the striking residence. It is located at 59 Cook Street and is named "Southern Mansions" despite having been built by a woman from Northern California, Christina Louise Haas.

— *Christina's Story* —

(AKA *Christina Louise Haas, Tina Haas*)

LIKE MANY OTHERS WHO STROLL BY 59 COOK STREET, I WAS ALWAYS intrigued with this house, especially with the added knowledge—gleaned from my former employer, the first city archivist, Ainslie Helmcken (who was a teenager at the time of its operation)—that it was built as a brothel. It is in an enviable location now, but at one time the area was decidedly not prestigious. Until the first two decades of the 1900s this Cook Street area and the surrounding neighbourhood known as Fairfield was marshland—not great for homes, but ideal for the many market gardens mainly tended by the Chinese population. A little farther into the neighbourhood was Smith's dairy farm. It all changed in 1907 when a large tract of land was sold to developers who created 171 lots and built extensive roads.[16]

One who saw the potential for a substantial house near to the park and yet still considered separate from downtown was a woman from California, Christina Haas. Christina was well versed in property development, having built hotels, acquired property, and invested in land in several coastal cities including San Francisco and Vancouver. She had money to finance a business and the experience to navigate the system to make it happen. She had a long, painful education with money right from an early age, but she developed business skills that served her well.

Although not completely alone, owing to her five siblings, Christina was orphaned when the death of her mother Johanna in 1866 when she was four was followed by a frightful shooting accident that took the life of her father Matthew when she was thirteen. Her parents had emigrated from Prussia in 1852 and made their way to California, where their children were born. A friend of the family who also come from Prussia, William E. Gerber, stepped forward to apply for guardianship at the request of the eldest son, John Henry. He placed the children into private board except for John Henry, who stayed in Mendocino. Gerber administered Matthew's considerable estate as a stock raiser, with in excess of 3,000 wool-producing sheep. As the estate began to depreciate Gerber petitioned to pay all creditors and sell the estate, which was accomplished in 1879.[17]

Administrator's Sale of Real Estate.

NOTICE IS HEREBY GIVEN THAT, IN pursuance of an order of the Probate Court of the county of Mendocino, in the State of California, made on the 21st day of July, A. D. 1879, in the matter of the estate of Mathew Haas, deceased, the undersigned, the administrator of the estate of Mathew Haas, deceased, will sell at private sale, to the highest bidder, for cash in United States gold coin and subject to confirmation by said Probate Court, on or after SATURDAY, the 16th day of August, A. D. 1879, at 10 o'clock A. M., all the right, title, interest and estate of the said Mathew Haas, deceased at the time of his death, and all the right, title and interest that the said estate has, by operation of law or otherwise, acquired other than or in addition to that of the said intestate at the time of his death, in and to all that certain lot, piece or parcel of land, situate, lying and being in said county of Mendocino, and bounded and described as follows, to wit: 1,680 acres of land situated in T 21 N, R 14 W, M D M, near Long Valley, in said county, and known as the "Haas Sheep Ranch;" also, all the personal property belonging to said estate, consisting of about 3,000 sheep, 5 horses and 3 cattle. Terms and conditions of sale, cash in gold coin of the United States; deed at expense of purchaser.

Bids may be made at any time after the first publication of this notice, and before the making of the sale.

All bids or offers must be in writing, and left at the office of W. E. Gerber, Auditor of Sacramento county, at his office in Sacramento City, or at the office of McGarvey & Carothers, attorneys at law, Ukiah City, Mendocino county.

W. E. GERBER, Administrator.

July 29, 1879.

McGarvey & Carothers, Attys for adm'r. 53t

Administrator's sale of the Haas Estate.
Matthew Haas Probate Papers, ancestry.com

Although it would seem a large estate, there were several creditors, and Gerber even complained he did not receive his full payment. Each of the children got their portion of $519.59 as they reached the age of majority; for Christina, that was April of 1880. Her sister Josephine had received hers a year earlier, and together they set up a store in Ukiah. It was a short-lived enterprise as Josephine died of typhoid fever in September of the same year, following their other sister Amelia, who had died of typhoid the year before.

Her only surviving sister, Annie, took her in, but then Christina is said to have lived and worked in several towns and cities in California, Nevada, Oregon, and Washington. Confirmation from primary records are few, but family notes with information passed on to the author indicate that she learned to make considerable money from her initial inheritance without appearing in many government records. The business of prostitution was a way to accomplish this if connections and following unwritten rules were the order of the day.

In 1899 Christina made her way to San Francisco, the epicentre for "the business," and like others had ambitions to make her fortune. She is said to have built a hotel/brothel in the Tenderloin district and through that made the acquaintance of two well-known madams in Victoria, Theresa Bernstein and Alice Seymour, who had their own connections to San Francisco.[18]

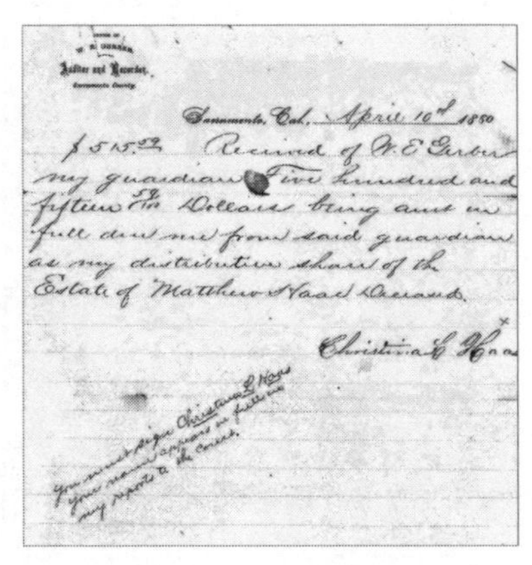

Sacramento, Cal. April 10th 1880

$515.59 Received of W. E. Gerber my guardian Five hundred and fifteen 59/100 Dollars being amt in full due me from said guardian as my distributive share of the Estate of Matthew Haas deceased.

Christina E. Haas

Christina's receipt, April 10, 1880. *Matthew Haas Probate Papers, ancestry.com*

She did travel to Victoria in 1902 and stayed for a few days; she then returned to her property in San Francisco but identified herself on the outgoing passenger list as a Canadian citizen. This may well have been to facilitate a return without questions.

She continued with investments and property ownership, possibly renting premises out for prostitution in San Francisco, when everything abruptly changed. At 5:12 AM on April 18, 1906, San Francisco experienced its most devastating earthquake and fires that levelled many buildings in the centre—particularly the Tenderloin. Some thought it was an act of God against evil, but in practical terms it meant years of rebuilding and huge financial losses.

After the San Francisco earthquake Christina had obviously accumulated money or financial backers as she built a hotel in 1908 in the Tenderloin—and possibly even a second one. It was likely exciting to be part of the rebuilding, but the amount of time and investment may have taken a toll on her finances and energy. She was now fifty years old and surely not ready to take on the battles of a serious moral reform movement. Victoria was likely still on her mind.

She returned to Victoria in 1912 and purchased the brothel of Alice Seymour at 715 Broughton Street, where she lived for a short time before renting it out. Soon after, she purchased two lots on Cook Street for cash and engaged highly successful local architect Thomas Hooper to design and oversee the construction of a beautiful classical revival home at a cost of $15,300, with touches that would lend themselves well to a high-end house.[19] Whether it operated for very long is doubtful, for a number of reasons.

At the time that Christina was living there she was surrounded by neighbours who were all connected to the real estate business and the neighbourhood building boom. The closest neighbour to her impressive house was William H. Logan at 97 Cook Street. He was a salesman with J.E. Smart & Co., and he had a twenty-two-year-old daughter and his wife residing with him. Next to him was Louis V. York, the president of J.E. Smart & Co., and his wife; around the corner at 1121 Woodstock Street was Herbert J. Knott, the president of Knott Bros. and Brown Real Estate Company. It may be expected that they knew how the house was to be used and likely disapproved of such an undesirable operation in close proximity.

There are accounts of neighbours recalling well-dressed women who worked there, but there are no reports in newspapers or police records to show any improper activity. It would seem from the small number of bedrooms (there were only three, with adjoining bathrooms) that it was intended to be for a very select clientele and a discreet operation, perhaps even an assignation house for consensual extra-marital affairs, which was a common sideline for the sophisticated carriage houses.

Two other major factors may have adversely affected Christina's ability to operate. First, the neighbourhood was rapidly developing as a location for families of some affluence. The houses and gardens were charming, the streetcar was extended, and many were now acquiring their own vehicles, so the idea of being out of town was no longer an issue. The horse racetrack had moved to the Willows area of Oak Bay, and even Beacon Hill Park was a more sedate place to pass the time.

Secondly, and perhaps an even greater factor, was that Christina's surname "Haas" was easily identifiable as of German origin. In May of 1915 the RMS *Lusitania* was sunk. Victorians rioted in the streets, attacking what they believed were German-owned businesses, some of long establishment, with widespread vandalism and looting. Business owners and individuals advertised in newspapers to distance their connection to Germany or German interests, but being perceived as aligned with Germany was an ever-present threat to many. At the height of the riots police were said to be powerless.

In 1919 Christina sold the house to John Day, the former owner of the Esquimalt Hotel. It was kept as the family home, notable for its gardens, until his death in 1944. The home was then renovated to become housing for returning military personnel after the Second World War.[20]

The same year as the sale, Christina returned home to Westport, California, to live with her brother John Henry and his wife Eva. Although she was alienated from some family members, Christina had always remained close to John and is said to have paid for his house. When John died, she moved into a home she bought from another family member and spent her last few years in the relative calm and quiet of Westport. She died in 1938 at the age of seventy-six and is buried at the Fort Bragg Rose Memorial Cemetery near to John Henry. Her will reflected the estrangement from some family, and she left a handwritten note:

> *Should anything happen to me I leave all my jewelry and possessions to my Niece Reba Haas. Any money left it is to be divided with Brother John Henry and Brother Charlie Haas after funeral expenses are paid. Some keepsake is to be given to Raymond Haas.*
>
> *I leave one dollar to any relative putting in a claim.*
>
> *Signed by*
>
> *Christina L. Haas.*[21]

No doubt Christina and Stella Carroll, who had left Victoria in 1915, were aware of each other's activities, but it is unknown whether they were acquainted. They certainly shared common life experiences, with the loss of their mothers at young ages. And in the end, they both found their business lives affected by the First World War. For Stella, it was after her return to San Francisco when a charge of treason was brought against her for operating a brothel within proximity of a military base, the Presidio; for Christina, it was the difficulty she faced in trying to operate a business in Victoria when carrying German ancestry and a German surname. For both women it was the end of their businesses, and both retired to properties in Northern California—Stella to a small rural property near Nice, and Christina to Westport. They lived ninety miles apart and died within five years of each other. I find myself wondering if they ever got together to reminisce about the old days. I will likely never know.

At the conclusion of the war, when the "boys" returned home, it was to a city whose streets were a little quieter and possessed of a little more decorum. Brothels still existed, as they do today, but discretion had become the key compromise with authorities. The city has changed with the times, and there have been shifts in social mores and the influence of public institutions like churches and civic organizations. Still, with all its complexities, the sex trade has remained.

59 Cook Street, Victoria, BC.
Photo by Linda J. Eversole

Christina Haas is buried with family members in Rose Memorial Cemetery, Fort Bragg, California. *findagrave.com*

Epilogue

NOT MUCH REMAINS FROM THE DAYS OF RAMPANT, OR AT LEAST more open, vice. The dance halls of the early days are all obliterated, as are the shacks of mysterious old Chinatown, now replaced with more substantial buildings of such note that the area is a national historic site and major drawing point for tourism.[1]

The old red-light district centred on Chatham Street was rebuilt for that purpose after the disastrous fire of 1907—but it soon dwindled in population, the cabins increasingly lived in by working men. Broughton Street in the 600 block is dominated by St. Andrew's Presbyterian Church, next door to a parkade, the site where Henrietta Morgan and Dora Son lay dying, just across from where Edna Farnsworth made the painful decision to end her life. Broad Street still has some of the old buildings that bore witness to the raucous laughter, staggering drunks, and occasional cat fights of the late nights, although these are largely from a later period.

Other grand old buildings have been lost. The saloons closed, the utilitarian cribs behind what was the Jubilee Saloon on Johnson Street torn down. Duck's Building, where Vera Ashton, Emma Johnson (Marval Conn), and Stella Carroll held a fatal Christmas

The boarded-up Jubilee Saloon cribs, ca. 1974.
Victoria City Archives M11386

dinner is in serious jeopardy from redevelopment. Stella Carroll's Herald Street house still stands, while the grand house Rockwood in Saanich was destroyed by fire in 1923. Other buildings from later periods that once housed rooms for prostitution as hotels or saloons still exist on lower Johnson Street and in various other places throughout the city. The former Dr. Hall's Restholme Sanitarium, built in 1885, is now a noted heritage house restored by a private owner.

> *Although some reformers called them the "lost sisterhood," prostitutes were not lost in their own communities. If they have become lost to history, it is because we have chosen to keep them*

> *invisible. In their own lifetimes they were not pathological individuals or passive victims, but actors in history who chose their occupation from a very limited array of alternatives.*[2]

With greater support systems through secular and non-secular organizations, and a growing awareness and acknowledgement of sexism in society, some of these stories may have ended differently in modern times. Changing attitudes and greater opportunities abound for women, yet change is still needed.

The women profiled here are just a few of the many who passed through Victoria. A lack of primary material and my own lack of cultural understanding precluded my including more in-depth stories on women from the Indigenous, Chinese, and Japanese communities in Victoria. I hope in time others will follow—those who can dig deeper and find equally compelling stories to join the ones in this book.

I also regret the lack of primary material on individuals who may have existed in the sex trade or were connected to it but whose records were not apparent. Material on same-sex prostitution, transgender people, and individuals who followed a path that would have been considered outside the norm seem not to have been demonized, but rather ignored.

In going through police records detailing charges and convictions in Victoria and Vancouver I found little reference save for a few arrests and convictions for homosexuality or cross-dressing. The incidents I did come across were in hotels when staff would report suspicions around two men sharing a hotel room. The attitude seemed to be if we do not acknowledge it, it doesn't exist.

Despite the lack of readily available resources to tell the stories of those denied a voice, continued and diligent research—and the sharing of the stories that emerge—can educate, enlighten, and recognize those who are a part of our history.

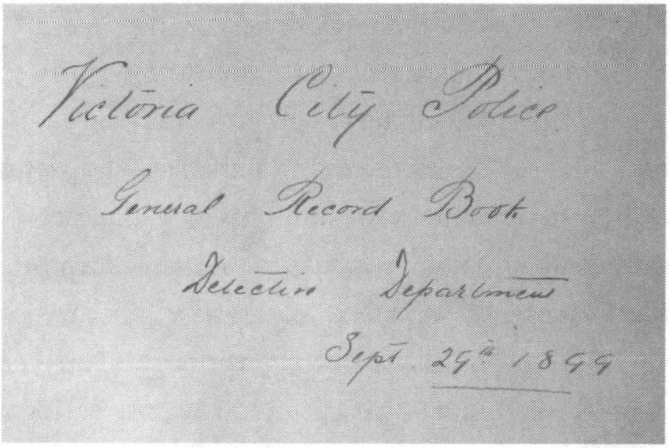
Victoria City Police
General Record Book
Detective Department
Sept. 29th 1899

Victoria Police Record Book flyleaf.
Victoria Police Museum and Archives

Acknowledgements

When there has been complex, comprehensive research invested in a project, it is hard to thank everyone who should be thanked. I have spent many years collecting the research used here, and my endnotes and bibliography don't reflect all the people who provided information and access to it. With technology has come the ability to confer with many people at far distances. Many I will never know personally. Without their help I could not have written this book. I have been in touch with numerous archives and museums, government offices, and their knowledgeable staff. There are far too many people to thank individually without running the risk of glaring oversights, but I am grateful to those who have shown interest and have brought material to my attention that I might have missed.

To the families who have shared their thoughts, mementos, and photos: I am thrilled that you consented to contributing and even more so that you care and value your ancestors, some of whom had challenging lives. It is important to know the stories of people who struggle and to see the strength and humour that carried them through. There is much to be proud of.

My special thanks to the team at TouchWood Editions, especially Taryn Boyd, Kate Kennedy, and Tori Elliott. You are a joy to work with.

To my own family and good friends whose love, interest, and encouragement spurred me on—especially my daughters Machala (editor extraordinaire) and Cheryl, who fill me with pride every day, I thank you. I must mention my late grandmother Cora Moody Menzies (1880–1949), WCTU member and suffragette, and her father Robert Moody (1859–1915), staunch Wesleyan Methodist lay preacher. I feel I can understand your world a little better.

Endnotes

CHAPTER ONE: FURS, FORTUNES, AND FANCY WOMEN

1. *British Colonist*, April 18, 1861, 2.
2. *British Colonist*, August 11, 1860, 3.
3. Valerie Green, *No Ordinary People* (Victoria, BC: Beach Holme Publishers, 1992), 92–95. Carey also worked as a land surveyor and owned several rural properties and real estate in Victoria. He was a landlord to brothel keepers. Carey Road, which led to his farm, is named for him.
4. *British Colonist*, December 25, 1861, 3.
5. BC Archives, GR-0848, Vancouver Island, Police and Prisons Dep't, Magistrates Charge Book Vol. 1, 1858–59, 22.
6. BC Archives, GR-0419, Dep't of Attorney General, Box 1, 1860, 19, R vs Na-Hor.
7. *British Colonist*, December 25, 1861, 2.
8. BC Archives, GR-0419, Box 3, 1864, 10, R vs. Charles King and Christopher Solburgh, David Hart testimony.
9. BC Archives, GR-0419, Box 3, 1864, 10, R vs. Charles King and Christopher Solburgh.

10. BC Archives, "Reminiscences of Philip J Hankin" E/B/H19A [Transcript] mf reel 119A(3), 53. For a time Phillip Hankin was the superintendent of police in Victoria.
11. BC Archives, PR-0124, Letterbook Volume 2, William Fraser Tolmie Fonds, noted in Chad Evans, *Frontier Theatre* (Victoria, BC: Sono Nis Press, 1983), 69.
12. *British Colonist,* August 10, 1863, 2.
13. Ibid.
14. Ibid.
15. Ibid.
16. *British Colonist*, August 14, 1863, 2.
17. Ibid.
18. Ibid.
19. Ibid.
20. *Stockton Daily Independent*, May 3, 1864.

CHAPTER TWO: CAPITAL, CONFEDERATION, AND "COMPANY LADIES"

1. Canada. *Sessional Papers*, "Report of the Royal Commission on Chinese Immigration," Vol. XVII, No. 2, 1885.
2. Ibid.
3. Ibid.
4. *British Colonist*, May 1 and May 20, 1876, 2.

5. *British Colonist*, June 13, 1876, 2, and June 22, 1876, 2.
6. Victoria City Archives, tax assessments, Victoria Directories, Vigelius, Ludwig.
7. *British Colonist*, December 15, 1876, 2.
8. Philip went to San Francisco, where he died in May 1870 in the Home for Inebriates. Sylvestria Smith, later Hastings, as a landowner is of historical note as the first woman to vote in an election, in the mayoralty race of 1875 in Victoria.
9. BC Archives, Joseph Bolduc and Martha Louisa Gillespie marriage registration.
10. "Capping" was not a commonly used term but may refer to soliciting and setting the price for a woman's services.
11. *British Colonist*, November 7, 1876, 2.
12. *British Colonist*, June 20, 1876, 3, and November 7, 1876, 3. Martha was brought up in Police Court on charges of taking household goods from Josephine Livingston for her own use.
13. BC Archives, Karl Mangims Dalbery and Martha Louisa Gillespie (Haley) marriage registration.
14. Canada 1881 Federal Census. According to this census Martha was living with Teresa Violand, Jennie Diehart, Jennie Bell, and Maude Branscombe. All were in their twenties or thirties while Martha was the eldest at forty.

15. BC Archives, inquest record, and *British Colonist*, October 28, 1883 and November 1, 1883. The newspapers refer to her as Lou Dolberry.
16. US Census 1900 and *British Colonist*, September 24, 1884. If Martha left Victoria before 1885, it is interesting to note that "C" [Carl/Karl] Dalberry was returning to Victoria from Puget Sound.
17. *St. Paul Republican* newspaper [Nebraska], June 22, 1905, 1.

CHAPTER THREE: LANDLORDS, LADIES, AND LOST SOULS

1. BC Archives, GR 1304.9803, Victoria Supreme Court, Probate, B08890 9 1481/1886, Henrietta Morgan.
2. Victoria City Archives, 1886, Bloomfield List of Houses of Ill-Fame (April).
3. BC Archives, Death Registration, Henrietta P. Morgan.
4. BC Archives, GR 1304.9803, 1886, Victoria Supreme Court, Probate, Morgan.
5. Canada. Census. 1891, Agnes B. Trachsler, widow who came to Canada in 1889.
6. *Daily Colonist*, August 4, 1889, 3.
7. BC Archives, MS-1143, Ancient Order of Foresters, Minute Books 1875–1968.

8. *Daily Colonist*, May 30, 1890, 5, and June 28, 1890, 5.
9. BC Archives Marriage Registration, Grace Harcourt and William Henry Jones, February 14, 1893; Birth Registration, Ida May Jones, December 17, 1895; Canada, 1911 Census.
10. *San Francisco Chronicle*, June 1889, quoted in James Nesbitt, "But People Wept When She Died" *Colonist*, June 7, 1964; also *San Francisco Daily Alta*, June 25, 1889. The *San Francisco Examiner*, June 25, 1889, identified her real name as Bruton.
11. San Francisco City Directory, 1888; California Voter Registration, 1888.
12. US 1880 Census.
13. BC Archives, GR-1327.425, BC Department of Attorney General, Inquest 34/89, Edna Farnsworth.
14. Census. England. 1871. John Croft was a medical student/practitioner as evidenced by newspaper reports and city directories.
15. BC Archives, GR-1327.425, BC Department of Attorney General, Inquest 34/89, James Douglas Helmcken testimony.
16. Ibid. John Croft testimony.
17. Ibid. Della Wentworth testimony.
18. Details on John's later years come from genealogical information on Ancestry.com, including Michigan directories, marriage and divorce records, and death registration.
19. Stockton State Hospital Record, No. 14742, George Jerome Farnsworth.
20. *Daily Colonist*, June 26, 1889, 3.

CHAPTER FOUR: BROADS, BUILDERS, AND BANKERS

1. Carroll Family Collection, Photograph, Duck's Block interior, December 1899.
2. Correspondence with Darcie Senf.
3. US Census Records 1850, 1860, 1870, 1880; New York State Census 1855.
4. Victoria City Archives Tax Assessments, Victoria City Directory.
5. *Daily Colonist*, February 21, 1890, 1, copied from *Seattle Times*.
6. *Daily Colonist*, February 7, 1892, 5.
7. *Daily Colonist*, September 22, 1892, 5.
8. *Daily Colonist*, November 26, 1892, 5.
9. BC Archives, GR1900, Chattel Mortgages, Volume 1, 551, Jean Ray to Dora Son. Jean Ray later operated a brothel at 130 Dupont Street in Vancouver.
10. *Daily Colonist,* January 25, 1898, 6.
11. Collis Brown was a British drug manufacturing company.

CHAPTER FIVE: IMMIGRANTS, IMPOSTERS, AND INMATES

1. Virginia Turner, Seattle Directory; Victoria City Archives, Tax Assessments, V. Truslove; BC Archives, marriage record, Fred Truslove and Virginia Turner; BC Archives, death record, Virginia Truslove; *Nelson Star*, January 19, 2014, article by Greg Nesteroff.
2. *Daily Colonist*, July 24, 1907, 2.
3. *Daily Colonist*, July 24, 1907, 1. Another significant event took place on this day: William J. Bowser was appointed as attorney general and would later order that any prostitutes or madams given jail time were to be turned out of the prisons or turned away at the door.
4. Information on the early life of the Johnson family comes from various sources on ancestry.com including birth and marriage registrations, directories, census records, and civil war records.
5. US 1880 Census.
6. US 1900 Census.
7. BC Archives, GR-1900, Chattel Mortgages, Volume 3, 727, 737, Vera Ashton to Marval Conn, Estella Durlin.
8. BC Archives, GR 1327, BC Attorney General Inquest, Marval Conn alias Ashton. The details of the death and the activities leading up to it come from witness testimony.

9. Findagrave.com, Old Vancouver City Cemetery, Vancouver, Clark County, USA, Johnson, Trullinger.
10. For further detail please see Linda J. Eversole, *Stella: Unrepentant Madam* (Victoria, BC: TouchWood Editions, 2005).
11. Postcard, Estella Carroll to Minnie Carroll, January 28, 1906, private collection.
12. Postcard, Minnie Carroll to Estella Carroll, March 16, 1903, private collection.

CHAPTER SIX: DETECTIVES, DEPORTATION, AND DEMIMONDES

1. BC Archives, Central Immigration Files, GR-1547 Volumes 569–70, White Slave Traffic Reports, 1909–1941, and Volume 478, American Prostitutes in Vancouver and Victoria, 1907–1910.
2. BC Archives, GR-784, British Columbia, Commission on Victoria Police Commissioners, 1910.
3. Ibid.
4. Ibid.
5. *Daily Colonist*, April 10, 1910, 2.
6. *Tampico Tornado,* October 1, 1887.
7. *Tampico Tornado*, April 2, 1887. Gray family information comes from ancestry.com, familysearch.org, interviews with family, and the Tampico Area Historical Society and Museum.

8. Maude's note to her sister is courtesy of Judith Whitt.
9. US 1900 Census.
10. Karen Abbott, *Sin in the Second City: Madams, Ministers, Playboys and the Battle For America's Soul* (New York, NY: Random House, 2007).
11. *San Francisco Call*, March 13 and 14, 1906, Trial of William F. Hopkins. *San Francisco Examiner*, April 28, 1906.
12. *San Francisco Call*, April 24 and 27, 1907, Trial of Roma Graham.
13. *San Francisco Call,* May 3, 1908.
14. *San Francisco Call*, November 2, 1908; *Vancouver Province*, September 18, 1913.
15. 1910 San Francisco Voter's List; *San Francisco Call*, September 9, 1909.
16. Vancouver City Archives, Building Permit No. 4674, Water Application No. 51437. The address number changed in several documents between 504 and 512.
17. BC Archives, Marriage Registration, Lillian Gray and Geoffrey Woodhouse, March 4, 1913.
18. *Vancouver Province*, September 12, 1913, 18–20.
19. *Province,* September 18, 2013, 1; BC Archives, Marriage Registration, Lillian Gray and Geoffrey Woodhouse; BC Archives, Divorce Index.
20. *Province,* September 24, 1913, 6.

21. Whitt, Judy to Linda Eversole, email correspondence, August 18, 2018.
22. *Daily Colonist*, September 24, 1889.
23. Hughes family information from ancestry.com, Washington directories, Washington marriage and birth records, US census records.
24. Newspaper reports for the *Vancouver Sun* and *Province* from September 9, 1912 and onward describe the story and wild west shoot-out.
25. BC Archives, GR1327, Inquest 222/14, Alice and Archibald Young, Sidney Petch's testimony.
26. BC Archives, GR1327, Inquest 222/14, Alice and Archibald Young, Victoria Police Detective Palmer's testimony.
27. *Daily Colonist*, May 13, 1914.
28. Patrick A. Dunae, "Geographies of Sexual Commerce and the Production of Prostitutional Space: Victoria, British Columbia, 1860–1914," *Journal of the Canadian Historical Association*, Volume 19, No. 1, 2008, 115–142.
29. Ibid.

CHAPTER SEVEN: THE REFORMERS

1. John Putnam, "Racism and Temperance: The Politics of Class and Gender in Late 19th Century Seattle," *Pacific Northwest Quarterly*, Vol. 95, No. 2, Spring 2004.
2. George H. Turner, *Before the Council or Social Life in Victoria*, February 1891. Augean Stables refers to the classical myth in which Hercules singlehandedly cleans out long-neglected cattle stables.
3. *WCTU Handbook*, 42, quoted in Lyn Gough, *As Wise as Serpents: Five Women and An Organization That Changed British Columbia, 1883–1939* (Victoria, BC: Swan Lake Publishing, 1988), 25.
4. John Endicott Gardner's name is spelled Gardiner and Gardner. Based on his own signature and legal documents I am using Gardner. He is occasionally identified with the name Vrooman. Vrooman was his stepfather, and he used this name at times to facilitate crossing borders.
5. *Daily Colonist*, July 13, 1888.
6. *Daily Colonist*, July 4, 1888.
7. Jennie Baldwin Hopkins lived with her mother in Oakland. In 1891 she married lawyer Walter Francis Shelley and later moved to Los Angeles.
8. *Daily Colonist*, July 13, 1888.
9. *Nanaimo Free Press*, June 16, 1889.

10. *Blaine Journal*, May 2, 1889.
11. *Seattle Post-Intelligencer*, July 30, 1896, 3.
12. Washington State Archives, Superior Court of the State of Washington for Whatcom County, Papers No. 4852, Menzies.
13. *Daily Colonist*, March 26, 1905.
14. Ernest A. Hall, *The Truth About Alcohol* (Victoria, BC: Free Lance Press, 1911), original available at Legislative Library of B.C.
15. *Victoria Times*, October 7, 1910.
16. Victoria Heritage Foundation, *This Old House: Victoria's Heritage Neighbourhoods*, Volume 4, Fairfield, Gonzales & Jubilee, 2009, 16.
17. Information on Christina Haas comes from correspondence with family members Mark T. Gowan and Earl Haas, Ancestry .com's death records for Christina and other family members, Matthew Haas probate records, census records, and passenger lists. The Mendocino County Historical Society reported a directory mention of Christina Haas owning 160 acres of land in that county in 1885.
18. US 1880 Census; correspondence with Mark T. Gowan including notes from Earl Haas.
19. Eve Lazarus, *Sensational Victoria: bright lights, red lights, murders, ghosts and gardens* (Vancouver, BC: Anvil Press, 2012).
20. Nick Russell, *Glorious Victorian Homes: 150 Years of Architectural History in British Columbia's Capital* (Victoria, BC: TouchWood Editions, 2016).

21. *Every Place Has A Story* (blog); "Christina Haas's Cook Street Brothel," by Eve Lazarus, posted February 8, 2014. Earl Haas, Christina Haas's relative commented on a story on this blog, providing information from his own research. Raymond and Reba are Christina Haas's nephew and niece. [This] "note (found among her possessions after her death) in her home just up the road from the old abalone Pub. Formally called the cobweb palace".

EPILOGUE

1. United Church of Canada: Toronto, Department of Temperance, Prohibition and Moral Reform, 33b, Minutes of the British Columbia Group of the General Board, 1914. Quoted in Patrick A. Dunae, *Geographies of Sexual Commerce and the Production of Prostitutional Space: Victoria, British Columbia, 1860–1914.*
2. Ruth Rosen, *The Lost Sisterhood: Prostitution in America, 1900–1918* (Baltimore: JHU Press, 1982), xiv.

Selected Sources

PUBLISHED

Abbott, Karen. *Sin in the Second City: Madams, Ministers, Playboys and the Battle For America's Soul*. New York, NY: Random House, 2007.

Adams, John D. *Old Square Toes and His Lady: The Life of James and Amelia Douglas*. Victoria, BC: TouchWood Editions, 2011.

Asbury, Herbert. *The Barbary Coast*. New York: Alfred A Knopf, 1933.

Backhouse, Constance. *Petticoats and Prejudice: Women and Law in 19th Century Canada*, Toronto: Women's Press, 1991.

Backhouse, Frances. *Women of the Klondike*. Toronto: Whitecap Books, 1995.

Barman, Jean. "Aboriginal Women on the Streets of Victoria: Rethinking Transgressive Sexuality During the Colonial Encounter" in *Contact Zones: Aboriginal and Settler Women in Canada's Colonial Past*, edited by Katie Pickles and Myra Rutherdale, 205–227. Vancouver, BC: UBC Press, 2005.

Barman, Jean. *French Canadians, Furs and Indigenous Women in the Making of the Pacific Northwest*. Vancouver, BC: UBC Press, 2014.

Barman, Jean. *On the Cusp of Contact*. Madeira Park, BC: Harbour Publishing, 2020.

Barman, Jean. *The West Beyond the West*. Toronto: University of Toronto Press, 1991.

Barnhardt, Jacqueline. *The Fair But Frail: Prostitution in San Francisco, 1840–1900*. Reno, NV: University of Nevada Press, 1986.

Baskerville, Peter A. *Beyond the Island: An Illustrated History of Victoria*. Burlington, ON: Windsor Publications, 1986.

Con, Harry, Ronald J. Con, Graham Johnson, Edgar Wickberg, William E. Wilmott. *From China to Canada: A History of the Chinese Communities in Canada,* Toronto: McClelland & Stewart, 1982.

Ding, Guo & Lai, David Chuen-yan. *Great Fortune Dream*. Halfmoon Bay, BC: Caitlin Press, 2016.

Dunae, Patrick A. "Geographies of Sexual Commerce and the Production of Prostitutional Space: Victoria, British Columbia, 1860–1914," *Journal of the Canadian Historical Association*, Volume 19, No. 1, 2008, 115–142.

Dunae, Patrick A. "Sex, Charades and Census Workers: Locating Female Sex Trade Workers in a Victorian City," *Social History*, Volume 42, No. 84. Toronto: York University, 2009, 267–297.

Evans, Chad. *Frontier Theatre*. Victoria, BC: Sono Nis Press, 1983.

Eversole, Linda J. *Stella: Unrepentant Madam.* Victoria, BC: TouchWood Editions, 2005.

Francis, Daniel. *Red Light Neon: A History of Vancouver's Sex Trade.* Vancouver, BC: Subway Books, 2006.

Gentry, Curt. *The Madams of San Francisco.* Garden City, NY: Doubleday & Co., 1964.

Gilfoyle, Timothy J. *City of Eros: New York City, Prostitution and the Commercialization of Sex, 1790–1920.* New York: W.W. Norton & Co., 1992.

Gough, Lynn. *As Wise as Serpents: Five Women and An Organization That Changed British Columbia, 1883–1939.* Victoria, BC: Swan Lake Publishing, 1988.

Gray, James. *Red Light on the Prairies.* Toronto: Macmillan, 1971.

Green, Valerie. *No Ordinary People.* Victoria, BC: Beach Holme Publishers, 1992.

Hall, Dr. Ernest A. *The Truth About Alcohol.* Victoria, BC: Free-Lance Publishing Company, 1911.

Hansen-Brett, Lacey. "Ladies in Scarlet: A Historical Overview of Prostitution in Victoria, British Columbia, 1870–1939." Essay prepared for Camosun College, 1984.

Ikebuchi, Shelly D. *From Slave Girls to Salvation*. Vancouver, BC: UBC Press, 2015.

Johnston, Susan J. "Twice Slain: Female Sex-Trade Workers and Suicide in British Columbia, 1870–1920," *Journal of the Canadian Historical Association*, Vol. 5, 1994, 147–166.

Lai, Chuen-Yan David. *The Forbidden City Within Victoria*. Victoria, BC: Orca Book Publishers, 1991.

Lazarus, Eve. *Sensational Victoria: bright lights, red lights, murders, ghosts and gardens*. Vancouver, BC: Anvil Press, 2012.

Lee, Erika. *At America's Gates: Chinese Immigration During the Exclusion Era, 1882–1943*. Chapel Hill, NC: University of North Carolina Press, 2003.

Lin, Cindy Che-Wen. "The History of the Oriental Home (1888–1942)," *McMaster Journal of Theology and Ministry*. Toronto: Emmanuel College, University of Toronto, 2016–17.

Lutz, John, et al. "A City of the White Race Occupies Its Place: Kanaka Row, Chinatown, and the Indian Quarter in Victorian Victoria," *The Routledge Companion to Spatial History*, Part III, Chapter 15. Abingdon, UK: Taylor & Francis Group, 2018.

Lutz, John. "After the Fur Trade: The Aboriginal Labouring Class of British Columbia, 1849–1890," *Journal of the Canadian Historical*

Association / Revue de la Société historique du Canada 3, no. 1 (1992), 69–93. https://doi.org/10.7202/031045ar.

Lutz, John Sutton. *Makuk: A New History of Aboriginal White Relations.* Vancouver, BC: UBC Press, 2008.

Marks, Lynne. *Infidels and the Damn Churches.* Vancouver, BC: UBC Press, 2017.

Marshall, Daniel. *Claiming the Land.* Vancouver, BC: Ronsdale Press, 2018.

Mofford, Glen A. *Aqua Vitae.* Victoria, BC: TouchWood Editions, 2018.

Morgan, Lael. *Good Time Girls of the Alaska-Yukon Gold Rush.* New York: Whitecap Books, 1998.

Moynahan, Jay. *Forty Fallen Women: Western Doves and Madams, 1885–1920.* Spokane, WA: Chickadee Publishing, 2008.

Moynahan, Jay. *Talkin' About Sportin' Women: A Dictionary of Terms Related to Prostitution on the American Frontier.* Spokane, WA: Chickadee Publishing, 2002.

Nesteroff, Greg. "Bealby Point (AKA Florence Park) Revisited," *Nelson Star*, January 19, 2014.

Putnam, John. "Racism and Temperance: The Politics of Class and Gender in Late 19th Century Seattle," *Pacific Northwest Quarterly*, Vol. 95, No. 2, Spring 2004.

Rosen, Ruth. *The Lost Sisterhood.* Baltimore, Maryland: John Hopkins University Press, 1982.

Russell, Nick. *Glorious Victorian Homes: 150 Years of Architectural History in British Columbia's Capital.* Victoria, BC: TouchWood Editions, 2016.

Smith, Curtis F. *The Brothels of Bellingham.* Bellingham, Washington: Whatcom County Historical Society, 2004.

Turner, George H. *Before the Council or Social Life in Victoria.* Victoria, BC: Department of Agriculture, February 1891.

Victoria Heritage Foundation, *This Old House: Victoria's Heritage Neighbourhoods,* Volume 4, Fairfield, Gonzales & Jubilee. Victoria, BC: Victoria Heritage Foundation, 2009.

Wolsey, Serge. *Call House Madam.* San Francisco: Martin Tudordale Corp., 1942.

GOVERNMENT RECORDS

British Columbia Archives: Vital Statistics Records, Wills and Probate Records, BC Attorney General – Documents and

Correspondence, Register and Indexes to Coroner's Inquiries and Inquests; Victoria Provincial Court Records; BC Provincial Police Records and Correspondence; Victoria Speedy Trials 1888–1916; Victoria Gaol – Prisoner's Charge and Sentence Book; Victoria Bills of Sale – Indexes and Registers, 1861–1956.

BC Archives, Central Immigration Files, GR-1547 Volume 569–70, White Slave Traffic Reports, 1909–1941 and Volume 478, American Prostitutes in Vancouver and Victoria, 1907–1910.

BC Archives, GR-784 British Columbia, Commission on Victoria Police Commissioners, 1910.

California State Hospital Records 1856–1923.

California Voter Registration 1866–1898.

Canada Census, 1871, 1881, 1891, 1901, 1911, 1921.

Canada. Sessional Papers, "Report of the Royal Commission on Chinese Immigration," Vol. XVII, No. 2, 1885.

US Census 1850, 1860, 1870, 1880, 1900, 1910, 1920.

US State Census, New York, Oregon, California, Iowa, Ohio, Illinois, various years.

Victoria City Archives: City Assessment Rolls, Directories, Minutes of Board of Police Commissioners, Magistrates Record Books,

Police Charge Books, Mayor's Reports, Fire Insurance Plans, Voter's Lists, Victoria, BC, Municipal Census 1871.

NEWSPAPERS

Bellingham Reveille

Blaine Journal

British Colonist (later *Weekly Colonist, Daily Colonist, Colonist,* and *Times-Colonist*)

Nanaimo Free Press

Nelson Star

New Westminster Columbian

Vancouver Daily World

Vancouver Province

Vancouver Sun

Victoria Daily Chronicle

Victoria Daily Times

Victoria Standard

San Francisco Bulletin

San Francisco Call

San Francisco Chronicle

San Francisco Daily Alta

San Francisco Examiner

Seattle Post-Intelligencer

Tampico Tornado

Whatcom Star

ONLINE

Ancestry.com (membership required): ancestry.com

Vancouver Public Library, BC City Directories: bccd.vpl.ca

British Colonist newspaper, 1858–1980: britishcolonist.ca

California Digital Newspaper Collection: cdnc.ucr.edu/cgi-bin/cdnc

Every Place Has A Story blog by Eve Lazarus: evelazarus.com/blog

FamilySearch (Mormon genealogy database): familysearch.org/en

FindAGrave (searchable database for gravesites and cemeteries in North America): findagrave.com

viHistory (source of historical census, directories, tax assessments for southern Vancouver Island): hcmc.uvic.ca/~taprhist/search/search.php

RootsWeb (genealogy site): rootsweb.com

BC-specific index on RootsWeb: sites.rootsweb.com/~canbc/index.htm

BC Archives Vital Statistics records: http://search-collections.royalbcmuseum.bc.ca/Genealogy

SFGenealogy (genealogy and history database for the San Francisco Bay area): sfgenealogy.org

University of Victoria Library's collection of Victoria Police Department charge books and mug shots: uvic.ca/library/featured/collections/about/VicPD.php

Victoria's Victoria index of historical Victoria newspapers: web.uvic.ca/vv/newspaper/index.php

Airing Victoria's Dirty Laundry (University of Victoria student project on prostitution in Victoria, BC): web.uvic.ca/vv/student/airingvictorias/home.htm

INTERVIEWS, CORRESPONDENCE

Carroll, John – Carroll family

Haas, Earl Mark Gowan – Haas family

Rood, Mary – Carroll family

Senf, Darcie – Son family

Tipton, Pam – Johnson family

Whitt, Judith – Gray family

REPOSITORIES

Most, if not all, the repositories listed below have online access to their digitized collections. Some work together and share the indexing, copying, and digitizing. Among these are the University of Victoria, the BC Genealogical Society, the Royal BC Museum and Archives, and the Victoria Police Archives. As this collaborative work continues the existence of pertinent resources will be more easily identified to the researcher, but much of their content remains limited to on-site visits. The scope of the original material is of great value to those wishing a deeper understanding of any given subject.

BC Archives

BC Genealogical Society

City of Victoria Archives

Mendocino County Historical Society

National Archives of Canada

San Francisco Library

San Francisco Museum

Tampico Area Historical Society and Museum

University of Victoria

Vancouver City Archives

Vancouver Police Museum & Archives

Vancouver Public Library

Victoria Police Archives

Washington State Archives

Washington State Library – Northwest Branch

Image Credits

Cover, ii–iii, 120, 121, 123: Gray family collection, used with permission

15, 20, 60, 70, 100, 171: Victoria City Archives, used with permission

19, 22, 29, 31, 45, 53, 62: *British Colonist*, used with permission

24: Canadian Methodist Historical Society, Rootsweb, public domain

48: Library of Congress, Map and Geography Division, public domain

56: ancestry.com, Gillespie Family Tree, *St. Paul Republican* newspaper, public domain

67: *Colonist*, used with permission

82, 111: Carroll Family Collection, used with permission

84: University of Victoria, public domain

90: *Daily Colonist*, used with permission

92, 95 (left and right): Paynter Family Collection, used with permission

93: Wikimedia, public domain

107: Pam Tipton Collection, used with permission

116 (top and bottom), 117, 138 (left and right): Vancouver Police Museum and Archives, used with permission

119, 173: Victoria Police Museum and Archives, used with permission

125: Library of Congress, public domain

128: Wikimedia, Library of Congress, public domain

135, 169 (right): findagrave.com

149: First Metropolitan United Church Archives, used with permission

163, 164: California US Wills and Probate records, 1850–93, Matthew Haas, ancestry.com, public domain

Index

Page numbers in italics indicate an illustration

A

Abson (Victoria police officer), 37

Ah Lin, 154

Ah Lun, 46

Ah Quay, 46

Ancient Order of Foresters, 64, 66–69

Anderson, John (Clarence Hotel), 87

Anderson, John (Lochend Farm), 54–55

Anderson, Robert, 54

Ashton, Marie. *See* Emma Johnson

Ashton, Vera, 12, 85, 105, 108, 170

B

Baker, Blanche Irene (Son), 86, 93–95, *94*, *95*

Baker, Charles F., 86

Becker, John, 47

Bernstein, Theresa, 164

Biggy, William J., 127

Bishop, Robert, 31, 35–38

Blanchard, Stella, 89

Bloomfield, Charles P., 59–61, *60*, 97, 152, 179

Bolduc, Joseph, 51, 54

Bowden, William, 46, 51–53

Bruton, Edna. *See* Edna Farnsworth

Burgess, J.P., 74

Burns, William, 18

C

Caledonia Sporting Grounds, 67–70, *70*

Callendine, Christian, 21

Cameron, John, 51–53

Cape Mudge, 16

Carey, Joseph Westrop, 15, 18–21, *20*, 61

Carroll, Stella (AKA Curtis, Durlin, Bearns, Fabian), 5–6, 12, 81, *82*, 100–01, 104–06, 108–114, *111*, 116, 119, 128, 130, 160, 168–69, 170–71

Central Union of Christian Endeavour, 147

Chi Kung Tong, 43–44

Chinese Rescue Home, 148–151

chlorodyne (drug), 90, 93, *93*

Clark, Robert Barr Dr., 62–64

Clay, Reverend Leslie, 91

Conn, Marval. *See* Emma Louisa Johnson

Connors, Tom (Jack), 65

Cook, Lizzie, *116*

Cooper, Rosalie. *See* Nettie Sager

Courtenay, H.C., 51–53

Cranshaw, Richard (AKA Richard Donovan), 28–40

Crease, H.P.P., 47

Cridge, Bishop Edward, 68

Croft, John, 75–77

Cruz, Mariano, 46

Curtis, Dudley, 110

D

Dalbery, Karl Mangims, 54

dance halls/houses, 8, 11, 23–28, 32, 42, 48, 87, 146, 170

Davis, Lewis, 30-38

Day, John, 167

Doane, Charlotte, 61

Doane, Joseph, 61

Doane, Margaret, 61

Douglas, James, 15–17, 22

Duck, Simeon, 47, 61, 80–82, 100–01, 104–05, 112

Duncan, George, 92

Dunsmuir, Robert, 91

E

Eastman, Franklin, 50
Elliot, Stella, 89
Evans, Ephraim, 23–24, *24*, 146
Evans, Olga, 123, 124
Everleigh, Ada and Mina (AKA Sims), 124

F

Farnsworth, Edna (AKA Bruton), 71–79
Farnsworth, George Jerome, 72–73, 77
Field Apartments, 140, *142*
Foster, Edward, 115
Francis, Lee (AKA Beverley Davis), 13

G

Gardner, John Endicott (AKA Vrooman), 149–154, *149*
Garrett, Reverend Alex, 10–11
Gerber, William E., 162–64
Gibbs, Dr. Joseph, 106–07
Gilbert, Dot, 75–76
Gillespie, Andrew and Temperance (Bankston), 11, 55–56, *56*
Gillespie, Martha (AKA Smith, Bolduc, Dalbery, Healey), 11, 48–56
Goodwin, Martha, 30, 34–35, 38–39
Graham, Lou, 87, 118
Gray, Lillian (AKA Roma Graham, Louise Grainger, Nellie Foster), 119–135, *119*, *120*, *135*
Greaves, Dr. George, 140–41

H

Haas, Christina Louise, 6, 161–69, *164*, *169*
Hall, Ernest Amos, 118, 157–59
Hall, Frank, 75
Harcourt, Grace (AKA Trachsler, Jones, Brown), 6, 64–71, 79, 88

Harcourt, Percy Danby (AKA Brother Sussex), 66–69
Hart, David, 24–25
Hastings, Thomas, 140
Hatton, Thomas, 75
Hayman, Jessie, 12–13, 11, 123–24
Haynes, Edith (AKA Belmont), 61, 63–64, 87, 90, 93
Helmcken, Ainslie, 5, 109, 169
Helmcken, James Douglas, 92, 93
Helmcken, John Sebastian, 2
Hooper, Thomas, 160, 165
Hopkins, William F., 11, 124–25
Hopkinson, William, 132
Hough, Constable, 55
Hughes, Alice. *See* Alice Young
Hunt, Claude, 89
Hunter, Gordon, 133

I

Immel, Henrietta, 26

J

Jackson, W., 55
Japanese Methodist Mission, 94, 95
Johnson, Charles Saxon, 101–03, 107, *107*
Johnson, Emma Louise (AKA Marval Conn, Marie Ashton), 12, 81, 101–08, 112, 170
Johnson, Jack, 127
Jones, Elmer, 132–33
Jones, Grace May. *See* Grace Harcourt
Jones, Ida May, 70
Jones, Louisa "The Countess", 89
Jones, William Henry, 69–70
Jubilee Saloon, 170, *171*

K

Kanaka, 17–18, 21–22
Kateka, 7, 18–19, 21

Ketchel, Stanley, 127–28, *128*, 132
Kruschke family, 144

L

Lampman, Judge Peter, 117–18
Langley, John, 100
Lee Toy, 106
Lewis, Gladys Adeline (AKA Serge Wolsey), 13
Lillooet, BC, 50
Littlefield, Frederick, 141
Loi Ho, 154
Lord, Maud. *See* Dora Son
Lush, William, 26

M

MacBride, Arthur, 25
MacCrae, Farquhar, 88
MacDonell, D.G., 133
Magnin, Victor, 126
Marston, Elvey, 87
Massoulle, Pauline, 58–59, 64
McAdams, James Reid, 25
McCartney, Billy, 138
McGinley, James, 124
McNaught, Joseph, 146
Mendoza, John, 25
Menzies, Jennie (AKA Hopkins, Shelley), 152–53
Menzies, Professor Walter Rufus, 148–157
Metcalfe (police officer), 25
Metropolitan Lodging House, 26
Miller, Andrew, 99
Mills, Samuel Perry, 59
Milne, Dr. George, 76
Ministerial Association, 147
Moore, Bessie, 130
Moral Reform and Temperance Association, 83, 89, *90*, 98, 144, 147, 155
Morgan, Henrietta (AKA O'Connor), 58–59, 61–63
Morley, Alfred, 116, 143, 147
Morris, Jennie, 96–98
Morrison, Aulay, 132–33

Morrison, Richard, 69
Moss, James, 51
Mulligan, James (AKA Reynolds), 128–29
Murdoch, Lizzie, 89

N

Na-Hor, 18, 21

O

Offerman, Fred, 90–91

P

Palmer, Thomas, 140–41
Parfitt Construction Company, 140
Park Hotel, 26
Pemberton, Augustus Frederick, 19–22, 31–38
Pemberton, Joseph Despard, 22
Perdue, George, 144
Petch, Sydney, 140
Pringle, Edwin H., 32–33
Pringle, Emma Jane, 30, 32–33
Purity League, 130, 147

Q

Quinn, W.H., 64–65, 77
Quong, 130

R

Ray, Jean, 90
Raymond, Pudgy, *117*
Reid, Malcolm, 132
Restholme Sanitarium, 158, 171
Ringo, Samuel, 22
Roberts, Martha, *116*
Robson, Premier John, 91
Royal Jubilee Hospital, 166–67, *167*
Russell, James, 53–54

S

Sager, Nettie (AKA Rosalie Cooper), 11
St. Andrew's Presbyterian Church, 83–84, 91, 170

St. Andrew's Roman Catholic Church, 83–84
San Francisco Earthquake, 99, 118, 133, *133*, 165
Scott, Mary, 137
Seymour, Alice, 83, 96–98, 164–65
Shakespeare, Noah, 45
Sheppard, Henry W., 88
Smith, Alfred William, 49–50
Smith, Andrew Wellington, 49–50
Smith, Harry, 55
Smith, Hector, 10
Smith, Martha. *See* Martha Gillespie
Smith, Phillip Robert, 49–50
Smith, Sophia (Martha's baby), 49–50
Smith, Sophia (later Eastman), 50
Smith, Sylvestria Layzell, 50
Smith, William, 49–50
Solbergh, Christian, 24
Son, Blanche. *See* Blanche Irene Baker
Son, Dora (AKA Maud Lord, Eldora Palmer), 85–96, *92*, *94*, *95*
Spalding, Hattie, 69
Star & Garter Saloon, 30–37, 42
Starr, Rev. John Edward, 78–79, 149, 152–53
Stone, Effie, 75

T

Toimoro, Karahue, 18–19
Tolmie, Alexander, 28
Tolmie, William Fraser, 28
Trachsler, Agnes, 64–65
Trimble, Dr. James, 51, 54–55
Trullinger, Charles Herbert, 103–04, 108
Trullinger, John Wesley, 102–03, 116
Turner, Virginia (AKA Truslove, Roberts), 98

V

Veyret, Rev. Monsieur, 9
Victoria Theatre, 34
Victoria Transfer Company, 12, 57–58, 74–75, 80, 84, 106
Victoria Voltigeurs, 22
Vigelius, Ludwig/Louis, 46–47
Voter's League, 147

W

Wall, Theresa, 12, 111, 113
Walls, John Patmore, 62–63
Watson, Fay, 90, 96–98
Weiler, Joseph, 62
Wentworth, Della, 13, 71–72, 74–75, 78
Wilmer, Police Officer, 37
Wilson, Lizzie, 89
Women's Christian Temperance Union (WCTU), 147
Woodhouse, Geoffrey Wilce, 131–32
Woodruff, Lena, 89

Y

Young, Alice (AKA Violet Vickers), 135–142
Young, Archibald, 135–142